D1606381

To:

_____

From:

_____

Date:

_____

STRONG &
Courageous

CHRISTIAN ART
PUBLISHERS

Published by Christian Art Publishers,
PO Box 1599, Vereeniging, 1930, RSA

© 2018
First edition 2018
Second edition 2023

Originally published in Afrikaans under the title *Moed vir elke môre*.
Translated by Therina van der Westhuizen.

First published in English under the title *Take Courage, Dear Heart*.

Designed by Christian Art Publishers

Cover designed by Christian Art Publishers

Images taken under license from Shutterstock.com

Printed in China

ISBN 978-1-77637-176-1 Faux Leather
ISBN 978-1-77637-177-8 Hardcover

23 24 25 26 27 28 29 30 31 32 – 10 9 8 7 6 5 4 3 2 1

Dedicated to:

my husband, Johan,
the person who gave me the courage
to start writing.

Introduction

Life requires courage on our part. It takes courage to get up in the morning, to do your daily chores, to maintain healthy relationships, to do the right thing. But what's more, it takes courage to be happy, to cry, to give and take, to love … and simply to survive.

Furthermore, to do His will, to obey Him and to bow down before Him often runs counter to human nature. And yet it is precisely this unconditional surrender and childlike dependence on our Creator that gives us the courage to get up every morning, face life and live it to the full. When the scorching sun of life burns down on our hearts, our strength can only be renewed when we go to our beloved Father. When loss and pain strip us of our will to live, He will embrace us in His loving arms.

During the wintery seasons of our lives, it is the knowledge that He holds us in the palm of His hand that gives us peace. It truly is through His grace that we develop the ability to complete life's journey with gratitude and joy.

May this book help you experience how God's Spirit gently carries and guides you through life. I pray that you may take hold of His hand, that you will have the courage to face every day and become all that you can be!

I would love to hear from you. Let me know what you think of the book or tell me about your own spiritual experience. You are welcome to contact me via email: mv@uppe.co.za.

~ *Milanie Vosloo*

January

The Courage to Start Over

Give the world the best you have, and the best will come to you.

~ Madeline Bridges

Many are the woes of the wicked,
but the LORD's unfailing love
surrounds the one who trusts in Him.

~ Psalm 32:10

Start Over

The LORD will keep you from all harm – He will watch over your life; the LORD will watch over your coming and going both now and forevermore. (Psalm 121:7-8)

The sparks of the fireworks have disappeared and we have to come to terms with the reality of the start-of-yet-another-year …

Maybe you are excited and look forward to what lies ahead. You have big dreams and are determined to stick to your New Year's resolutions. Or you feel uncertain and doubtful about what lies ahead as if you're standing at the foot of yet another seemingly unsurpassable mountain. Whatever the case may be, there is one thing that you can be sure of: your Father will accompany you every step of the unknown way.

When you truly trust Him and make Him a part of your life, He will be your Protector, your Guide and your Confidante.

Take hold of His outstretched hand and pray that the Spirit
will convince you of the fact that He will once again guide you
safely: every moment of every day for the rest of your life!

*Here I am, Creator, I am strong and courageous because I am not alone.
Thank You for never leaving nor forsaking me. Amen.*

Do Not Fear

"Do not be afraid of them, for I am with you and will rescue you,"
declares the LORD. (Jeremiah 1:8)

I have old confidantes with whom I can just be myself. With them, I can be honest about how I feel and say things like: "I feel discouraged … happy … excited … hurt … scared …" I know that I can trust them.

Because we know each other well, we know that we all feel a little doubtful at the beginning of a new year. We discuss questions like: "What do you think awaits us this year?" Yet we also know that sometime during our conversations, God will answer and say, "I, the Lord God, will take care of you …"

Dear friend in Christ, it is quite normal to have doubts and even to despair at the beginning of a brand-new year. Fortunately, our Father knows us all too well, He knows our deepest feelings and His Word promises time and again that He will never forsake us.

Alexandre Dumas said, "Life is fascinating: one just has to look through the right glasses." This year, look at life through the lenses of courage because you know who goes before you.

Thank You, faithful God, that You – the One who maintains the entire universe – are also my Father! Amen.

Take Him at His Word

Now faith is confidence in what we hope for and assurance about what we do not see. (Hebrews 11:1)

When life has disappointed you, it is really hard to trust with all your heart again. When it comes to promises, we always seem to wonder where the catch is. The wonderful truth is that – regardless of the fact that people are fallible – God is faithful for all eternity. Yes, you can take God at His Word and believe Him when He says:

- "You will be My people, and I will be your God" (Jer. 30:22).
- "My grace is sufficient for you, for My power is made perfect in weakness" (2 Cor. 12:9).
- "Do not fear" (Lam. 3:57).
- "God is protecting you by His power until you receive this salvation" (1 Pet. 1:5, NLT).

Take your Father at His Word every day of this
New Year. He is already taking care of you!

Thank You, Master of my life, that Your promise to care for me always remains true. Amen.

JANUARY 4

He Is with You

God said to Moses, "I AM who I AM. This is what you are to say to the Israelites: 'I AM has sent me to you.'" (Exodus 3:14)

God can change our lives in the blink of an eye. Just like with Moses. He was just a simple shepherd going about his menial daily business when all of a sudden God Himself appeared to him and said: "So now, go. I am sending you to Pharaoh to bring My people the Israelites out of Egypt" (Exod. 3:10). What an overwhelming responsibility!

Maybe this coming year's responsibilities, duties and challenges seem like a long winding road through the desert to you. Maybe you also feel like stutteringly telling God that you really are not up for the challenge and that He should rather send someone else, to make your life easier. It may happen that God asks you to take on a great responsibility this year.

So when you stand there, hesitant to start your journey through the desert, remember that God Himself – the great I AM – will go before you. It doesn't matter how hard the life-road ahead seems, He is already there.

Look out for God's pillar of cloud and pillar of fire in your life. Follow it and know for sure: the God-Who-is-God is with you.

I will follow You, my Guide, unconditionally. Amen.

Take Life Step by Step

Little by little I will drive them out before you, until you have increased enough to take possession of the land. (Exodus 23:30)

We all struggle to be patient at times. We want things to happen quickly, our problems must be sorted out at once and we want our dreams to realize overnight. When these things don't happen straight away, we become frustrated and our impatience often leads to feelings of despair.

Just like the Israelites, we are quick to complain to God when things don't go the way we want them to when we want them to. God, however, will not be rushed. Just like He drove out the enemies of the Israelites little by little, He is working in our lives bit by bit, because He knows exactly when we are ready for what. All projects, buildings and periods start with the first step, the first brick, the first minute.

When this principle is in place and you do your part to trust God, you can be sure that He will make everything work out perfectly.

Allow God to guide you through life step by step.

Lord, please teach me to wait patiently and to trust that You will work everything for my good in Your time. Amen.

Follow His Lead

And He passed in front of Moses, proclaiming, "The LORD, the LORD, the compassionate and gracious God, slow to anger, abounding in love and faithfulness." (Exodus 34:6)

Having God in our lives does not mean that we will necessarily be exempt from pain, discomfort, stress and suffering. If it worked like that, everyone on earth would probably be believers. However, your life changes radically when you surrender it to Him, because then you belong to the Father. And because we are His children – He promises to take care of us like a Father.

He promises that His grace will cover us like a cloud every moment of every day – grace that says: "My arms are around you, I am in you and I go before you, My child. Every moment of every day. You can trust Me, knowing that I will show you the way."

If your life belongs to the Father, you can be confident in every step that you take. His love for you is inexplicable – you are His beloved child – and He will never leave you to fend for yourself.

Heavenly Father, I put my hand in Yours. Please guide me through this day and every day of this year. Amen.

Radical Change

"Your Father in heaven [will] give the Holy Spirit to those who ask Him!" (Luke 11:13)

Your life changes radically when you accept God into your heart and choose to have a personal relationship with Him. Once you have done that, the Holy Spirit dwells in you and He enables you to become more and more like Jesus every day.

If you want to make the best of the year ahead, follow this golden rule: listen to and obey the Spirit of God that lives inside you. If you do this, your life will be different in so many ways because it won't be about you anymore, but about doing what He asks of you. Making this change is not easy, but it is definitely worth it.

Jesus has an invitation for you today:
"Come and experience the joy there is in living the way
God wants you to. It is not difficult to do; to be
honest, once you start living like this, you will realize
how wonderful life really is" (see Matt. 11:29).

Lord Jesus, I want to live the way You expect me to. Please help me to do that. Amen.

Be Different

When Moses came down from Mount Sinai with the two tablets of the covenant law in his hands, he was not aware that his face was radiant because he had spoken with the LORD. (Exodus 34:29)

We all know that chameleons are enchanting creatures. These little animals have the amazing ability to change color. They have a wide spectrum of colors suitable for any situation.

You and I are very much like chameleons. Our lives give others a clear indication of where our hearts are at. When someone is far from God, others can see, hear and feel it in the way that they behave.

Fortunately, people can also clearly sense it when someone's heart is anchored in God. After spending 40 days with God, Moses' entire being visibly bore the evidence. We read that his face shone because being in God's presence had changed him; he was different.

Dear friend, be still and pray that the Spirit will come and renew you today so that your life will reflect God's great glory.

Lord, come and live in me. Fill me. Become one with me so that other people can see You in me every day. Amen.

Live a Life That Is Different

"My dwelling place will be with them; I will be their God, and they will be My people. Then the nations will know that I the LORD make Israel holy, when My sanctuary is among them forever." (Ezekiel 37:27-28)

Your Father loves you with an everlasting love. And that is why He wants to change you. When you allow the heavenly God to touch your life, you will never be the same again. Throughout the Bible, we find and are utterly amazed by the accounts of how the Spirit came and completely changed people's lives around.

For instance, Zacchaeus was transformed from a dishonest tax collector into a kind and generous man after meeting Jesus. Timothy believed with all his heart when Jesus who was crucified stood before him in person. Peter's life changed radically when Jesus appeared to him after His resurrection. Saul, who initially persecuted Christians, became one of the most devoted followers of Christ – he became Paul, an icon of our faith.

> What about you? How did your life change
> the day that you answered Christ's call?
> Did it become new? Are you now living a life
> that is *different* from the one you lived before?

Father God, please renew my mind so that I can think and live differently. So that I can live like a child of Yours should. Amen.

Make Him a Priority

Whoever watches the wind will not plant; whoever looks at the clouds will not reap. (Ecclesiastes 11:4)

The year has just begun. We feel like we can take on any challenge and many of us have long lists of things that we want to do this year. The question, however, remains: are you equally excited about your spiritual journey … or does it not really appear high up on your list of priorities?

Dear friend-in-Christ, nothing that you take on, do or accomplish can ever be as important as laying a solid foundation and growing spiritually.

Throughout the history of the church, believers have found that activities like memorizing and meditating on the Bible, fasting and praying, seclusion and study, celebration and worship, suffering and confession have proven invaluable in helping people to better see and understand the truth of God.

Have you set your spiritual goals for this year?
What about for the rest of your life? Are you
sticking to your plan to achieve those goals?

Lord of my life, show me what You expect of me and give me the courage to be obedient to You. Amen.

Enjoy His Fountain of Life

"Whoever drinks the water I give them will never thirst. Indeed, the water I give them will become in them a spring of water welling up to eternal life." (John 4:14)

Have you ever had the privilege of spending a few minutes at a quiet stream or a gushing waterfall? Can you recall God's peace flowing through your being as the water babbled down the brook? How far removed you felt from the daily grind and the typical challenges and noises of the rat race? Or how you felt the tangible presence of the Spirit?

Even though most of our time is spent worlds apart from such idyllic tranquility, we can still take a moment and experience the rest there is to be found in God's love and presence. His fountain of peace is only a thought away. Therefore, we can – in the midst of the stressful hustle and bustle – find complete peace knowing that the headspring of His love serves as a never-failing fountain of life for us.

Allow the Spirit's living waters of peace to fill you all day, every day.

Holy Spirit, flow through me like a constant stream so that I can feel Your love today and share it with others who thirst after Your living water. Amen.

Be Enthusiastic

"And I will ask the Father, and He will give you another Advocate to help you and be with you forever – the Spirit of truth."
(John 14:16-17)

Children have the wonderful ability to become ecstatic about seemingly small and unimportant things, to spontaneously burst out in laughter and to get totally lost in their make-believe worlds. Unfortunately, we lose a lot of our enthusiasm and spontaneous joy when we are "all grown up" and the responsibilities of life get the better of us.

Our Father truly wants us – His precious children – to live with a joyous, expectant hope. And that is why He gives us His Spirit of joy every day. The Spirit enables us to once again find joy, despite all of life's disappointments, failures and bitterness. Yes, through Him, you can still have childlike enthusiasm, in spite of it all.

Pray and ask the Spirit to cleanse your life of every little
bit of negativity so that you can once again experience
pure love and joy. Start to rejoice and get excited about
the big, and small, miracles in your life right now!

Holy Spirit, please take away whatever keeps me from living my life with joy. Amen.

From Strength to Strength

For none of us lives for ourselves alone, and none of us dies for ourselves alone. If we live, we live for the Lord; and if we die, we die for the Lord. So, whether we live or die, we belong to the Lord.
(Romans 14:7-8)

Did you know that your thoughts determine your life? That you have the ability to either attract positive or negative things and people? If you keep thinking and believing that only bad things will come your way, you are right.

However, when you agree with the Spirit and focus on the positive things and believe that God has the best in store for you, then you are also right. God really does want to work all things for your good. That's why He wants you to live as a positive person.

He equips you, every day, to be fulfilled, happy and successful; to be His child and happy to be alive.

Allow the Spirit to fill you with His positive love every
day and pray that your thoughts will be His thoughts.
Then Proverbs 11:28 will become evident in your life:
the righteous will thrive like a green leaf.

Father, thank You that I can live a life of abundance with You. Amen.

Believe That You Can

"And I will do whatever you ask in My name, so that the Father may be glorified in the Son." (John 14:13)

Do you believe that you are destined to lead a happy and fulfilled life? Do you believe that God has big dreams for you and that you can do anything through Him who strengthens you?

Do not allow your negative thoughts about yourself and your life to become a stumbling block. Ask the Spirit daily to help you believe that you can live a successful and positive life with – and through – Him. Believe that you can do all things with God by your side.

Make Him part of every thought and dream for your life and you will be amazed at what you can accomplish.

> Make Solomon's wisdom your own today: "In all your ways submit to Him, and He will make your paths straight. Do not be wise in your own eyes; fear the LORD and turn away from evil" (Prov. 3:6-7).

Father God, let my thoughts be Your thoughts so that I can be positive and happy. Amen.

Live a Fulfilled Life

To this you were called, because Christ suffered for you, leaving you an example, that you should follow in His steps. (1 Peter 2:21)

We all know that material things only offer us a limited amount of fulfillment and that all worldly recognition and pleasures are fleeting.

And so we sometimes cannot help but wonder: what do I need to do to live a truly purposeful life? Peter gives us the answer to this question in 1 Peter 2:22-25 – it is to follow in Jesus' footsteps:

- He never sinned.
- When people hurled their insults at Him, He did not retaliate;
- He was content to entrust everything to God.
- He never did anything to displease God.

Jesus lived the perfect life. And through His death, He atoned for our imperfections. Therefore, by His grace, we should follow in our Master's footsteps every day.

Pray that you will have the courage to follow Jesus' example today. It will give your life meaning and purpose.

Lord Jesus, I can only do Your will with Your help. So please help me. Amen.

Be Remembered

I say to the LORD, "You are my Lord; apart from You I have no good thing." (Psalm 16:2)

We would all like to be remembered. After all, none of us think that our existence is so meaningless that we have not made a difference in some way. Some of us want to be remembered for our accomplishments, our ground-breaking work or the new records we set. Others hope that people will remember them for their prestige, riches or status.

What do you want to be remembered for? It is an important question to consider as it determines, to a great extent, what you will spend your energy and time on as well as what you will use your talents on.

Maybe the words of William Bridge will help you find the answer to this all-important question: "Seek not great things for yourselves in this world, for if your garments be too long, they will make you stumble; and one staff helps a man in his journey, when many in his hands at once hinders him."

Work to do great things for God and He will do great things for you.

Ask God to show you what He wants you to be remembered for.

Lord God, what legacy am I to leave behind? Amen.

Leave a Legacy

If we live, we live for the Lord; and if we die, we die for the Lord. So, whether we live or die, we belong to the Lord. (Romans 14:8)

It is great and honorable to strive towards leaving behind a legacy; something to leave to the generations to come. The world surely would have been a lot poorer without the legacy of Thomas Edison who invented the light bulb, Alexander Graham Bell who developed the telephone, Isaac Newton's law of gravitation, Shakespeare's words or Churchill's valor.

Just think how poor we would have been without the life of our Lord Jesus Christ. Not only did He give His life for us, but He also left us His blameless example to follow. Centuries later, He is still remembered for the way that He lived, how He changed people's lives and for how He gave all of Himself for the sake of humankind.

Jesus forsook Himself because He wanted to leave behind a legacy of the Father's love for all people on earth.

Would you like to be remembered for the
way that you lived your life for the Lord?

Great God, I want to do what You created me for: to live in such a way that others will be reminded of You! Amen.

Love God

... keep yourselves in God's love as you wait for the mercy of our Lord Jesus Christ to bring you to eternal life. (Jude verse 21)

The Gospel can be summarized in one word: Love. It is out of love that the Creator made us, it is because of His great love that the Son came to save us and it is the Spirit of Love that accompanies us every day.

Our God loves us so much that He spends every moment of every 24-hour day right by our side, putting His great arms of compassion around us, holding us tightly.

When we start to comprehend a bit of the vastness of the Father's love, we cannot help but to respond with love in return. It makes our hearts overflow with thankful love and then we want nothing more than to honor Him in everything we do and say. Erich Fromm said, "Love is an act of faith, and whoever is of little faith is also of little love."

If your faith in God is unshakable, then you will find it easy to love Him, yourself and those around you. Then you will constantly want to cry out: "Lord, I love You so much!"

My God, I really truly do love You. Please teach me how to make the love that I have in my heart visible through the way that I live. Amen.

Love Yourself

These commandments and whatever other command there may be, are summed up in this one command: "Love your neighbor as yourself." (Romans 13:9)

It sounds so easy: love yourself. But is it as easy as it sounds? To be honest, most of us often devalue ourselves, recall our mistakes and exaggerate our weaknesses.

Yes, as women we sure do excel at lovelessly chastising and criticising ourselves. The fact of the matter is that we simply cannot love others unconditionally if we cannot accept and embrace ourselves with love.

"A baby is born with a need to be loved", said Frank A. Clark, "and never outgrows it." Only God, through His Spirit, is able to nourish and water this plant of love inside of us so that it can grow. When that happens, our self-love develops into a caring love that enriches other people's lives as well.

Make the decision to love yourself unconditionally today. You may. Because God loves you unconditionally too!

Teach me, Lord, to care for myself so that I can love others as well. Amen.

Find Rest in Love

If I have the gift of prophecy and can fathom all mysteries and all knowledge, and if I have a faith that can move mountains, but do not have love, I am nothing. (1 Corinthians 13:2)

After retiring from tennis, Boris Becker said that he had everything; from flights on the Concorde to accommodation at the very best hotels. Everything except love. And he was lonely.

How ironic that so many people just keep searching all their lives, because they pursue everything but love. There is only one way to find inner peace and true fulfillment and that is to live a life of love: love for God, for ourselves and for others.

Love gives an ordinary life an extraordinary sense of meaning. St. Augustine said, "Love is the fulfillment of all our works. There is the goal; that is why we run: We run toward it, and once we reach it, in it we shall find rest."

Have you found true rest? That rest that makes it abundantly clear that you love your Father, yourself and others unconditionally?

God of love, teach me how to express Your kind of love toward others. Amen.

Love Wholeheartedly

"As the Father has loved Me, so have I loved you. Now remain in My love." (John 15:9)

God wants us to be people of love. For that reason, He gives us ample examples of what sincere love should look like in His Word. James 3:17 teaches us the following about people who love:

- Such a person will live in peace with others.
- He or she does not step on other people, but takes their feelings into consideration.
- Such a person is not obstinate or difficult to work with.
- He or she readily forgives others.
- He or she does nice things for others without expecting something in return.
- No matter what he or she does, it will always be for the benefit of others.
- You will always know where you stand with such a person.

Our human tendencies of selfishness and stubbornness naturally oppose a heart of love. Let us pray continually that we will become less and that He will become more.

Thank You for covering me with Your love so that I am able to cherish others. Amen.

Make a Difference

But whoever looks intently into the perfect law that gives freedom,
and continues in it – not forgetting what they have heard, but doing
it – they will be blessed in what they do. (James 1:25)

Do you ever wonder if you make any difference in this world? If your life has any kind of impact on others at all? If your presence makes a difference to your family or your co-workers?

Yes, my dear woman, you do make a difference. Many years have gone into preparing you – your person and your life – to do exactly what you are doing right now. The reason that you find yourself where you are, is to make a difference. Ask yourself the following questions: Is the difference I'm making a positive one? Do my presence and my contribution bless others? Do I express Jesus' love? If you answer "yes" to these questions, then you are doing exactly what God expects of you. If, however, you are uncertain, then it is still not too late. You are given yet another opportunity to change your heart, thinking, words and actions with every new sunrise.

Pray and ask the Spirit to teach you how to make a
life-changing difference in the lives of those around you.

Lord Jesus, will You please help me to be a blessing to others? Amen.

Answer When God Calls

Moses said to God, "Who am I that I should go to Pharaoh and bring the Israelites out of Egypt?" (Exodus 3:11)

God calls you for a special purpose. Something that will ask a lot from you and that you do not feel up to at all. How will you respond to Him? Wouldn't you, like Moses, also wonder if you misunderstood Him? Would you not also be tempted to come up with excuses and resistance?

God uses ordinary people in extraordinary ways. So therefore, He can call anyone, anywhere in any way that He wishes so that He can have His purposes fulfilled. He may even have a particular task for you this day, this month or this year. He might want you to be of service to Him in a special way. Do you have the courage to answer yes when He calls?

Open your heart daily so that you can hear God's
voice when He calls and pray that when He wants to use
you, you will not hesitate to say, "Yes, Lord, use me."

Spirit of God, I wait on You. Call on me and make me willing to do Your will. Amen.

God Is with You

"I will be with you. And this will be the sign to you that it is I who have sent you: When you have brought the people out of Egypt, you will worship God on this mountain." (Exodus 3:12)

God will never ask anyone to venture into the deep end without giving them a safety jacket. When He assigns a certain task to you, He will surely also equip you for it. So, you never have to doubt yourself when the Spirit has shown you that you must do something. Your almighty Father's great, supportive hand will help you do it.

Consider this today: Has God called you to do something in the past? What was your answer? Do you think He has a special task for you this very day, or this month or this year? When God calls people, He is serious about getting them to take the road He wants them to go. Remember that the task He gives you is also very important to Him and so He vows to walk with you all the way.

Take God's hand, follow where He leads
and do what He asks. You can do it!

How fortunate am I that You would take my hand and tell me: "I will be with you". Amen.

Remain Obedient

You were bought at a price; do not become slaves of human beings. Brothers and sisters, each person, as responsible to God, should remain in the situation they were in when God called them.
(1 Corinthians 7:23-24)

It's easy to be enthusiastic about something when you're just starting out. But it becomes somewhat harder to keep it up when we are met with resistance, when we become lazy or tired. Yes, children of God often have to overcome obstacles on their road of obedience. Moreover, the world often also tries to convince us otherwise.

Dear friend-in-Christ, read today's passage from Scripture again. Allow the Spirit to convict you anew of what you must do, how you should live and what it is that God expects of you. Then lay down your entire life before Him and ask Him to help you stay obedient and faithful.

Pray that you will have the conviction and perseverance to serve Him as you ought to.

Today, remember: God is with you!
Therefore, you can do all things!

Heavenly Father, I sometimes feel so vulnerable and weak. Please strengthen me, guide me and stay with me … all day. Amen.

Be Brave

Have I not commanded you? Be strong and courageous. Do not be afraid; do not be discouraged, for the LORD your God will be with you wherever you go. (Joshua 1:9)

God always equips His willing children in His service with exactly what they need for a specific task. Just as He blessed the stammering Moses with knowledge and wisdom during the entire journey through the wilderness, He also assured Moses' successor, Joshua, of His faithfulness right from the start. And because Joshua was courageous, he became Moses' worthy successor who led the people into the Promised Land.

As God appointed Joshua, He encouraged him with the following words: "As I was with Moses, so I will be with you; I will never leave you nor forsake you. Be strong and courageous ..." (Joshua 1:5-6). History has proven again and again that God is faithful to His children and that He equips and strengthens those whom He calls.

If God has called you, be brave! He will go before
you and make your way secure and steadfast.

Thank You, Lord of my life, that I can trust You with my life. Amen.

Look Ahead

May the LORD your God be with you ... be strong and courageous!
(Joshua 1:17-18)

Quite often we are our own worst enemies. Despite knowing what we are supposed to do and being deeply convinced that God is faithful, we are sometimes afraid of moving forward.

It is at times like these that we are like the Israelites who were not willing to move because the road ahead was unknown (and most likely uncomfortable). It is almost as if we feel that it is much safer to return to the familiar past, just like the Israelites longed for the meat pots of Egypt.

Obedient children of God don't keep looking back. They move forward, trusting God, because they know that He is with them. So, if you have been given the command to do something, to move on ... then go. You know that your God will never leave nor forsake you.

Remember, you can't live fully today if you are stuck in yesterday. Look ahead and move forward.

Father, please give me the courage to meet the future, knowing that You are by my side. Amen.

Let the Walls Come Down

When the trumpets sounded, the army shouted, and at the sound of the trumpet, when the men gave a loud shout, the wall collapsed …
(Joshua 6:20)

God's instructions were simple. The Israelites were to invade Jericho without the use of weapons. All they had to do was march around the walled-in city once every day for six consecutive days and on the seventh day, they had to march around Jericho seven times while the priests sounded the trumpets. "Then," said the LORD, "the wall of the city will collapse and the army will go up, everyone straight in" (Joshua 6:5).

God's instructions may sometimes seem strange. And it's usually then that we do what we think is right … just to realize later on that our own "clever" plans didn't work. The truth found in Scripture is that God can make the impossible happen when He is fighting for you. Like making the walls of resistance collapse at the sound of a trumpet …

When God is on your side, you need not fight.
All you need to do is to obey Him.

Thank You, Lord, that I know You can also make the walls in my life come down. Amen.

Be Victorious

The LORD said to Joshua, "Do not be afraid of them; I have given them into your hand. Not one of them will be able to withstand you." (Joshua 10:8)

Being devoted to God implies that you obey Him. And when you faithfully follow Him, you can be sure that He will make miracles happen in your life. Like on that day at Gibeon when Joshua and his men had to fight the Amorites.

Joshua and his army knew that they would need more than one day to conquer the enemy. So, they asked God to make the sun stand still so that that one day would be as long as two. And God did it! In order to help His people achieve victory, He made the sun stand still for an entire day!

If you are obedient to your Father, you can relax. He can, and will give you miraculous victories according to His will.

Live today safe in the knowledge that nothing and no one can do anything to your heart when God is on your side.

Master of my life, I praise You because You are so great. Amen.

Make the Best of Every Day

When you were dead in your sins ... God made you alive with Christ.
(Colossians 2:13)

Do you also sometimes get bored with your dull life? Then you wonder if there is any point to your daily routine. Or if your ordinary life has any meaning.

The answer is yes. Your "ordinary" life does have meaning and you will see it when you start to think differently about your life. You will see things in a new light when you realize that nothing should be taken for granted. Then you'll be able to find great joy in even the most menial of tasks. When you start to look at every dull task in your daily routine with grateful eyes, you'll soon spot the miraculous in everything and your feelings and attitude will start to change.

Be truly alive today by focusing on the privilege of having friends, the love of your family, the beautiful sunrise ... and even the sparkly bubbles in the "ordinary" dishwater!

> Live today, and every day of this year, according to
> these words: Choose to make the best of every day
> and in so doing, add deeper meaning to your life.

Lord, please give me the courage to find joy in my everyday life. Amen.

Keep the End in Sight

This is the verdict: Light [Jesus] has come into the world, but people loved darkness instead of light because their deeds were evil.
(John 3:19)

Some days may loom like an unsurpassable mountain before you. You wonder how you will ever get the things done on your to-do list and to be honest, you don't even really feel like doing any of it.

When you feel this way about what lies ahead, remember one thing – this too shall pass. Every task will eventually come to an end, every big assignment will be completed at some point and every uphill has a downhill.

Don't only focus on the dark tunnel ahead of you, but keep your eye on the ray of light at the end of it … then do your part and watch as the light becomes larger and brighter. Amid all the ups and downs, remember to keep the Light always before you. The fact that God is working alongside you, turns mountains into molehills and pitch-black tunnels into bright and easy thoroughfares.

The Light brings us the truth and
illuminates our path in life. See Him today!

Light of my life, here is my hand. Take it and please lead me every step of the way. Amen.

February

The Courage to Truly Be a Woman

We are all bowed instruments in the symphony of God's joy.
His Spirit plucks at our heart strings
and then it starts to sing His praises.

~ Jacob Boehme

The Lord is compassionate and gracious,
slow to anger, abounding in love.

~ Psalm 103:8

Be a Happy Woman

And the God of peace will be with you. (Philippians 4:9)

As women we tend to postpone happiness. Just listen to the conversations among women. The one will complain about her job and believes that she will be happier when she quits. Another will say that her life will be better if she could just lose some weight. A third hopes to escape her marriage so that she can re-discover herself and yet another is annoyed with her teenage children. It often goes like this, we bemoan our lot.

It is true that many women have more than enough reasons to feel miserable, but maybe next time we can try to steer the conversation in a new direction. Maybe we should talk about reasons for being happy and grateful. Surely there is always something to be grateful for and that brings joy – despite circumstances.

Decide to be happy today – no matter what your situation.
You'll be surprised at how much joy life really does have to offer.

Father, please help me to be a grateful person that is happy with my life. Amen.

Give Your Worries to Him

Cast all your anxiety on Him because He cares for you. (1 Peter 5:7)

Most of us know that God can solve our problems in ways that we can never imagine. We have also learnt through experience that if we leave things up to Him, He will give us the answers to our prayers at just the right time.

Unfortunately, human nature turns us into slaves of anxiety! All too often we allow stress and worry to get the better of us. But time and again, God proves to us that He is faithful; that He will never forsake us and that He will always take care of us.

Let's pray that God will change our hearts of little faith into hearts of unshakable faith and that He will teach us the art of really trusting Him. Furthermore, let's pray that He would assure us of His goodness and omnipotence so that we can put all our cares in His hands … and leave them there.

With the help of the Spirit, you can develop the ability
to be a worry-free child of the Most High.

O Lord, it is so wonderful that I am able to have peace of mind by trusting You! Amen.

Address the Small Issues

Since we live by the Spirit, let us keep in step with the Spirit.
(Galatians 5:25)

Isn't it ironic? We are often able to handle the big issues with patience and gracefulness, but then we allow the small leaks to sink our lifeboat!

We are so focused on courageously addressing and sorting out the difficult challenges, that we are just not up to dealing with the small stuff. We are very good at handling all the problems and people at work with great self-control and then … the moment we set foot in the door at home, we lose our cool.

Well, when God said that we should bear the fruit of the Spirit, He meant that we should always do the right thing in all circumstances. We can only do this if the Holy Spirit is in total control of our emotions, words and behavior.

Today, pray to be incessantly filled with
the Spirit. It will be the silent power that
will stop even the smallest of leaks.

Please forgive my weaknesses and let Your Spirit take control of my life. My entire life, Father. Amen.

Live with Self-Control

So I say, walk by the Spirit, and you will not gratify the desires of the flesh. (Galatians 5:16)

Everything in our life can run smoothly for weeks. We feel in control of our emotions and we even succeed in maintaining love and peace in our relationships with others. And then one day … we don't feel good about ourselves, things go wrong unexpectedly, and other people keep pushing our buttons.

It is then that we throw our proverbial toys out of the cot. We lose our temper, say the wrong things and behave in ways that fill us with shame and regret. When we are truly committed to maintaining peace and love in our relationships with others, such outbursts are embarrassing and make us feel bad about ourselves. After all, we know that such behavior is not in God's will and only causes unnecessary damage.

There is no quick-fix to a lack of self-control. We are all fallible human beings. But with our Father's grace we can always repair the damage to relationships by asking for forgiveness and receiving it. Then we can start over and keep striving to live a Spirit-filled life.

Father, please help me to keep the good things intact and to mend what I have broken. Amen.

Remember to Whom You Belong

Rejoice in the Lord always. I will say it again: Rejoice! (Philippians 4:4)

We are very quick to forget. Even though we have heard it a thousand times over: God loves us and we are His precious children; but we forget it the moment that life is tough. We tend to only see the negative in everything and we paint a grim picture of all that's wrong in our lives.

Today, remember that the heavenly Father selected you to one day sit next to His throne. Keep in mind that He promises in His Word that He will not leave you alone for even a moment, that through Him you can handle any situation and that He wants to embrace you with His arms of unfailing love. Take the words of Philippians 4:19 to heart: "And my God will meet all your needs according to the riches of His glory in Christ Jesus."

> Dear friend, remember to whom you belong.
> Then your heart will not be able to contain the joy.

Lord, please help me to realize what it really means to be Your child and remind me to live my life in utter reliance on You. Amen.

Be Happy with Yourself

For we are God's handiwork, created in Christ Jesus to do good works, which God prepared in advance for us to do. (Ephesians 2:10)

We struggle to accept ourselves just the way we are. We often wish that we could change just a few things about ourselves. Some women want to be shorter, others want to be taller, some want to be blonde and others want to pick up weight, while most of us are fighting the figurative battle of the bulge. We want to be more beautiful, clever and rich. So as a result, we go through life constantly wishing to be different and feeling dissatisfied with ourselves.

Imagine how very different life would be if you could just make peace with yourself. If you could just accept who you are. What a massive difference it would make to your attitude towards life and your level of happiness!

Make the decision to be happy with how, what and who you are. Do it today. Then flash a smile at life that says, "I am content!" You are at your best when you are truly you.

Thank You, Creator God, for creating me and making me beautiful. Please help me to be ME. Amen.

Nourish Your Soul

"Remain in Me, as I also remain in you. No branch can bear fruit by itself; it must remain in the vine. Neither can you bear fruit unless you remain in Me." (John 15:4)

A woman's soul really needs a lot of care and attention. Despite all the wonderful things we can do, we are simply more sensitive, vulnerable and delicate than our male counterparts. The truth is that each of us bears the personal responsibility for that part of our being. Irrespective of whoever or whatever demands our attention, taking care of our soul is a must! When we neglect our souls, it affects all the people in our lives and everything around us.

You should ask yourself how many minutes per day you spend taking care of your soul. How much time do you spend delving into His wonderful Word and making it your own? How often do you talk to the Spirit while you go about your daily routine? Does God know that you love Him, that you are grateful and that you honor Him because you constantly thank and praise Him with all your heart?

Every aspect of your life will change when you take care of your soul. Then you will truly be a woman who is alive.

Spirit of God, I want to honor You with my whole life. Amen.

Remember What Life Is All About

"Martha, Martha," the Lord answered, "you are worried and upset about many things, but few things are needed – or indeed only one [and that is to know God]." (Luke 10:41-42)

Women are always busy. It is as if we just don't have the luxury of doing nothing for a while. There is always something or someone that requires our attention. Is this limited to our era only, or is it some self-imposed female "thing" that has been part of womanhood through the centuries?

Well, when I read the Martha-Mary story in Luke 10, it seems to me that this tendency to be too busy is something that has always been part of being a woman. It might be because we constantly feel responsible for everything and everyone, or because we honestly want to make everyone around us happy. Or maybe we are trying to prove our own value through busyness.

This story makes it very clear that if our lives are too busy, then we run the risk of forgetting what life is really all about.

Lord, please help me not to lose myself, and You, in the hurry-scurry of my life. Amen.

Make the Right Choices

"Few things are needed – or indeed only one. Mary has chosen what is better, and it will not be taken away from her." (Luke 10:42)

Jesus' words really must have brought Martha to a standstill. Wasn't she the one who was doing everything in her power to serve others? And now Jesus tells her that her sister – who was doing nothing but sitting at His feet – had made the better choice. That only time spent with Him has eternal value!

You and I both know what it is like to have an infinite list of responsibilities that compels us to always operate in seventh gear. But listen carefully to what Jesus tells you today: "Never get so busy that you don't have time to sit at My feet. Because what I have to offer you lasts for all eternity!"

Life is all about making choices. Make the decision to change your way of life today so that you will have enough time to pay attention to the things that really matter in life: like quiet time with the Lord, prayer and Bible study.

Lord Jesus, help me to settle down so that I can hear Your voice. Amen.

Take Care of Your Body

You are not your own; you were bought at a price. Therefore honor God with your bodies. (1 Corinthians 6:20)

If there is one thing that troubles us as women, it is the constant struggle to look good. Just listen to the conversations women have over coffee. It's not long before we start talking about appearance: what we look like (and what we want to look like), how we struggle with our weight (and what we wish we weighed), what new hairstyle we're going to try (in an attempt to feel better about ourselves) or what outfit we're planning to wear to some or other function (so that we can compare favorably with the other guests).

Yes, a woman's physical appearance is important. The fact that your body is a temple that the holy God indwells, really makes it worth the effort to look after yourself.

Remember the Arabic proverb that says:
God is on the side of those who persevere with
patience. And continue to look after yourself.

Bridegroom, please help me to sanctify my body for You in a balanced way. Amen.

Just Be You!

Humble yourselves, therefore, under God's mighty hand, that He may lift you up in due time. (1 Peter 5:6)

Sometimes when I page through magazines and admire the models' perfect bodies, flawless skin and beautiful faces, I think to myself: "How nice to know that you look like a supermodel." And then … I read the stories of how these "perfect" women's lives are often falling apart, because they are just ordinary people with needs who also have to face the demands of everyday life – just like you and me. Then I realize that it is indeed important to look after my body, but that I cannot attain happiness – or eternal life! – by looking like a supermodel.

Our Creator does want to see us nourish our bodies and souls with the same amount of dedication and care. Finding the balance between our physical appearance, our earthly needs and our spiritual lives is a challenge that we will have to contend with as long as we live in our "earthly tent".

Pray that the Spirit will give you the wisdom
to love your whole being with kindness.

Thank You, Lord, that I don't have to be perfect to be a child of God. Amen.

Enjoy Your Spouse

But since sexual immorality is occurring, each man should have sexual relations with his own wife, and each woman with her own husband. The husband should fulfill his marital duty to his wife, and likewise the wife to her husband. (1 Corinthians 7:2-3)

According to Scripture, sex is meant to be enjoyed by both parties inside of marriage. What a wonderfully liberating passage! It clearly tells us that there is a connection between our spiritual lives and our sexuality. Yes, God really does want us to fully enjoy the sexual aspect of being human as well!

It is His gift to married couples! When you are married, sex is one of the most important aspects of your life and not just a typical honey-moon experience.

God created us as sexual beings so that we can give ourselves to one another in marriage. When you give yourself to your spouse, you are in God's will and fulfilling a part of the purpose of being a woman.

Enjoy your spouse – also on a physical level. Because you can!

Father God, thank You for the fact that I may enjoy my husband's body. Amen.

Fulfill All Your Roles

Teach slaves to be subject to their masters in everything, to try to please them, not to talk back to them, and not to steal from them, but to show that they can be fully trusted, so that in every way they will make the teaching about God our Savior attractive.
(Titus 2:9-10)

The woman is the heart of every family; her husband and children's lives revolve around her and oftentimes women are also the steadfast ones in the workplace. Women are able to sense what other people need and then they do something about it.

They are mainly concerned with other people's interests and often push their own needs to the back burner. Give a woman something to do and it will get done … because women assume responsibility for all their roles and they are dedicated, loyal, honorable and reliable. Jesus knew that women have these qualities and that is precisely why He gave women recognition and showed the world why women need to be honored in a time when they were considered inferior to men. Today, He still has infinite understanding and compassion for women.

You can be sure of this today: Jesus notices you!
He sees the dedication and passion with which you
fulfill every role. And today He wants to tell you:
"Well done, dear woman. I am proud of you!"

Thank You for noticing everything I do, Lord! Amen.

Set the Right Example

We are therefore Christ's ambassadors, as though God were making His appeal through us. (2 Corinthians 5:20)

Women, and especially mothers, are particularly well-suited to the task of portraying Jesus' character here on earth. Our Father gave us very specific qualities to enable us to show the world what His love looks like. Yes, your eyes are not deceiving you. The way you live shows the people around you, those at work and at home, what a great God you serve. What a wonderful honor and what a massive responsibility!

Ask yourself today: do I live my life in such a way that others can see something of my Master in me? Do other people know that I talk to Him on a regular basis? Do my children see me reading His Word and do they learn to pray by hearing me pray? Am I showing them how to make Jesus part of their lives? Do others follow Christ because of the example that I have set?

Pray every day that the love of Jesus
will manifest itself through your life.

Savior God, please help me in my weakness as a human being to emulate Your image of love more and more every day. Amen.

Strike a Balance

For physical training is of some value, but godliness has value for all things, holding promise for both the present life and the life to come. (1 Timothy 4:8)

Women sometimes say to one another, "You know, I always have to be everything to everyone." And yes, that's true, the fact that we often have to singlehandedly manage and do so much, can get to us. I mean, we also get tired and we would also like to be spoilt a little every now and then.

I've learnt from experience that there is only one person who can make sure my life is balanced: me! I am the only one who can ensure that my needs are addressed – amid all the responsibilities that come with being a woman. It is my responsibility to make quiet time with the Lord a priority and to schedule time for relaxation.

So, I want to encourage you to see yourself as a priority. Make time for the things that are important to you. Make time to just be a woman.

Amid all our roles as mothers, daughters, grandmothers, friends, employees, spouses, lovers … it is important to find time to enjoy being a woman. You deserve it.

Comforter God, please teach me the art of striking a balance! Amen.

Be Your Own Kind of Clever

My frame was not hidden from You when I was made in the secret place, when I was woven together in the depths of the earth. (Psalm 139:15)

Do you sometimes feel silly? I sometimes feel that way when I'm in a conversation where people are discussing topics I know nothing about, or when people reel off numbers so large that I can't even wrap my head around them. It is easy to feel intimidated in the company of people who are gifted in areas that you are not.

In actual fact, there is no need for us to feel like that. We all have some unique form of intelligence. There are those with exceptional musical abilities or mathematical skills, while others have linguistic intelligence. Others have excellent ball sense and others have spatial intelligence so they just never get lost. Of course, there are also those people who get along very well with everyone (emotional intelligence). The fact of the matter is: we are all born with one or other type of intelligence. For that reason, we never have to feel inferior.

Cherish, appreciate and develop your own cleverness!
That is what sets you apart and makes you special.

Forgive me, Master, for selling myself short. Amen.

Live Wisely

The mocker seeks wisdom and finds none, but knowledge comes easily to the discerning. (Proverbs 14:6)

Do you know what is really stupid? Not when you can't do math or when you can't catch a ball, when you struggle to master a new language or when you sing out of tune. People are really stupid when they think that they are clever enough to make it without God's wisdom and grace. According to Solomon, that is utter foolishness!

Maybe you read through yesterday's devotion and as you went through the different forms of intelligence, you wondered which apply to you. Think about it carefully, because you do have at least one kind of intelligence.

When you develop your abilities and use your talents in conjunction with God's wisdom, you will be twice as good as what you are on your own. Then you are capable of so much more and you will be a success – in His eyes at least!

Pray and ask God to cover you in His divine wisdom
every day. Then you will live a fulfilling life!

Let me experience the riches of Your wisdom today, Father. Amen.

Enjoy His Approval

For it is not the one who commends himself who is approved, but the one whom the Lord commends. (2 Corinthians 10:18)

One of the reasons why we sometimes sell ourselves short to please others is because there is a part in all of us that is seeking other people's approval. Let's be honest, we really do want other people to like us and to hold us in high esteem.

But now the Word tells us something quite different. It says … all that matters is that God approves of us. Isn't that a relief? The fact that we are only accountable to Him takes away a lot of stress and self-imposed feelings of guilt. So, you can stop trying to please everybody. If you do try to please everybody, the chances are that you won't impress anyone … and you will be an infinitely unhappy person.

In every situation, ask the following: "God, what do You want me to do?" And then when He answers you, do exactly what He tells you to do. That is all that really matters.

Holy Father, help me to seek and to enjoy Your approval above all. Amen.

Live a Sensational Life

The grace of our Lord was poured out on me abundantly, along with the faith and love that are in Christ Jesus. (1 Timothy 1:14)

Do you see every day, week, month and year as just another period of time that you want to put behind you as soon as possible? Do you think that life is nothing more than your job, the grocery shopping that you still need to do, the finances that must be sorted out and raising the children? Do you consider your existence to be a series of responsibilities that you need to get through just so that you can tackle the next thing on your to-do list?

If that is the case, you are most probably not enjoying life. Because you are not experiencing all the facets of your God-given life. Close your eyes for just a moment and feel your own breath, feel the temperature around you, feel the emotions in your heart … feel what it feels like to be alive!

Become aware of the fact that you are
alive today. Don't just do things mindlessly.
Feel and live life – all of it. It is sensational!

Father, please forgive me for sometimes seeing my life as a dismal duty sheet. Please teach me the art of being truly alive! Amen.

Enjoy Your Job

Whatever your hand finds to do, do it with all your might.
(Ecclesiastes 9:10)

Our day jobs can sometimes get us down. To expect that we should jump out of bed every morning with a song on our lips and be all excited about everything that we have to do today, is surely not realistic.

Sometimes, our jobs can be extremely demanding, the daily grind can wear us down and then we just get tired … and at times even feel discouraged. To dislike your job from time to time is probably quite normal, but if you are permanently negative about your daily stint and the environment in which you work, it might be time do to some introspection.

Ask yourself what it is that makes your job so unbearable. Is it because you are not with the right organization, or because the people you work with get to you, or because you simply don't enjoy doing what you're doing, or because you are exhausted and possibly burnt out? You are the only one who can analyze your unique situation and get to the correct answers with your Spiritual Companion's help.

God does want you to enjoy your job. Ask Him how.

Dear Leader of my life, please show me the way. Amen.

Open Your Purse

This is how it will be with whoever stores up things for themselves but is not rich toward God. (Luke 12:21)

There are two reasons why we work. The first is to earn money and the second is to be able to enjoy it. God enables us to work and to make money so that we can enjoy it. Success and prosperity are not evil per se. Actually, it is a God-given privilege. What is, however, important is how we earn the money and what we do with it.

If you earn your bread and butter in an honorable way and if you spend your money sensibly, the Father has no problem with wealth. What He does ask of us, though, is not to spend our income on ourselves alone, but also on other people and His Kingdom. God gives to you so that you, in turn, can give to others.

> Do you give enough of your privileges and income back to God? Where, how and to whom do you think can you give more?

Giver of good gifts, I want to give more back to You. Show me where, how and how much. Amen.

Give Your Heart

[God] comforts us in all our troubles, so that we can comfort those in any trouble with the comfort we ourselves receive from God.
(2 Corinthians 1:4)

What would the world be like without the gentleness of female hearts? Yes, women have a radar system specially designed to pick up on other people's pain and we have the special ability to put all of our hearts into drying those people's tears.

Henri Nouwen wrote: "To console does not mean to take away the pain but rather to be there and say, 'You are not alone, I am with you. Together we can carry the burden. Don't be afraid. I am here.' That is consolation. We all need to give it as well as to receive it."

Let's be women of consolation. Women who are so deeply aware of God's gracious comfort in our own lives that it causes us to spontaneously wipe away other people's tears. Because when we comfort others, we tend to forget all about our own heartache.

Thank You, Comforter, that You are always there to assure me of Your loving care. Show me how and where I can share it with others today. Amen.

Enjoy God's Goodness

He said, "Throw your net on the right side of the boat and you will find some." When they did, they were unable to haul the net in because of the large number of fish. (John 21:6)

Peter felt like going fishing. So he and a few other disciples decided to go out onto Lake Tiberias in the hope of catching a few fish for supper. But what a disappointment! The poor, hungry men had not even caught one fish by sunrise. Until Jesus told them what to do … and they caught so many fish that they couldn't even haul their nets back into the boat! On top of that, Jesus was waiting for them on the shore with a fire already going and some fish grilling on it. What a wonderful treat!

When our hearts are tuned in to the Holy Spirit's guidance and when we do what He asks us to, then God gives in excess. We will not be able to "haul in" all the blessings that He bestows on us so abundantly.

Obey God's voice and you will be surprised at the
amazing fires-of-grace that He lights in your life.

Thank You, God-full-of-goodness, for the grace overflowing in my life. Amen.

Drink from His Cup

When I said, "My foot is slipping," Your unfailing love, Lord, supported me. (Psalm 94:18)

You are most probably a woman who just gives: someone who is always there for other people, who help where you can, offer support to those around you and you selflessly give of yourself. It is because you are a woman that you like to share your love and everything about you with others. You are like God's mouth, hands and feet here on earth. And for that reason, your Father rejoices over you!

But … women also run the risk of being left empty because they are always giving! There may come a time when there is nothing left because you've given so much of yourself to others. It is, therefore, very important to always refill your life-cup at the Source, your Father. Even with all the demands that others make on you, you need to spend some special time with Him. Remember Leo Tolstoy's words: "He is that without which one cannot live."

> There is One whose goodness never runs out. It is the One who continually wants to fill you with His love from the cup in His heart that overflows.

Father God, thank You for giving me abounding love. Amen.

Be Cherished

*The LORD is gracious and righteous; our God is full of compassion.
(Psalm 116:5)*

Love that cherishes is the kind of love that a mother has for her baby;
the love between a young couple in love; the love of a dear friend who
cares deeply for you … and the love that the Father has for you! Yes,
God's love puts its tender arms around you, lifts you up in His hands
and looks at you with great kindness.

Are you allowing God to cherish you? Or are you so busy to "do
everything yourself" that you don't even give Him a chance? Maybe
you are missing out on God's tender love for you precisely because you
are so independent and self-reliant.

Close your eyes for a few minutes and focus only on your
Father. See how He picks you up to sit on His lap, how He
puts your head on His chest and hear how He whispers in
your ear: "I love you, My child, so very, very much."

Thank You, my dear Lord, for embracing me with so much love. Amen.

Drink in His Tender Love

The LORD is compassionate and gracious, slow to anger, abounding in love. (Psalm 103:8)

How can we experience God's love in our lives? How can we be able to feel His love … when we can't even see Him?

- We become still. Absolutely silent. We even quiet our thoughts.
- We pray and ask the Holy Spirit to fill us with His presence.
- We wait patiently … until we feel that we have made a true connection with Him.
- Then we listen … until we hear and feel His love flowing over us.
- And then we gratefully start drinking in every drop of His tender love.

Make time throughout your day to drink deeply of your Father's cherishing love and to enjoy the peace that it brings. In this way, you will find rest despite the unrest; in spite of the bustle of the world, you will feel content and experience how He fills you with peace that surpasses all understanding.

Remember: He loves you more than words can say!

Lord God, I want to drink in Your love today and experience Your glory with every sip. Amen.

Be an All-Out Woman

Teach me Your way, LORD, that I may rely on Your faithfulness; give me an undivided heart, that I may fear Your name. (Psalm 86:11)

Your entire life can change in the blink of an eye. And for that reason, it is important for us women to live all-out every day. You may ask: what should a woman do to live all-out? Well, I think it depends on every individual and how she wants to live her life and what makes her inner being brim with excitement. There are, however, also a few universal things, that are related to womanhood, that make us feel different. Making time to reflect, to love, to be friendly, to laugh often, to give with a happy heart, to pray in all sincerity, to work hard and to do God's will.

The number of years we live is less important than the quality of the life that we live. As women, let us reach out and touch others with tender hands, look at them with compassionate eyes and encourage them with our wise words.

Let's plant and regularly water trees of joy in our hearts so that others can enjoy the fruit we bear.

Lamb of God, I want to live every day as if it is my last. Will You please help me to do so? Amen.

Reach Out

"Blessed are the merciful, for they will be shown mercy."
(Matthew 5:7)

Life can really leave people beat and broken down. The world has mistreated many and a lot of women live in truly terrible and depressing circumstances. You and I are here to reach out to the broken ones who have been used and abused by life. Yes, in spite of your own circumstances, you are always able to do something meaningful for someone else. All you need to do is to open your eyes, your ears and most of all … your heart.

Do you know someone who is suffering? Maybe someone you work with, someone in your community or church. Someone in need of something that you have to offer … financial support, a helping hand?

Maybe someone would really appreciate your company. You could offer them a patient ear, a gentle heart, a friendly smile, a loving touch … or even forgiveness.

> You are a woman. So that means you have a heart that is tender enough to heal other people's pain, a heart that is strong enough to strengthen them, and big enough so that they can feel at home in it. Be that woman today!

Lord, I am at Your service, please use my womanhood for Your glory today. Amen.

Take Him with You

For the message of the cross is foolishness to those who are perishing, but to us who are being saved it is the power of God.
(1 Corinthians 1:18)

Sometimes the continual struggle to keep moving forward, while the waves of life crash all around us, leaves us tired and feeling hopeless. In the sea-of-life, we are sometimes overwhelmed by massive waves and at other times, we seem to be merely bobbing up and down in one place. It is during exhausting times like these, that we usually try to row our lifeboat all on our own; without the Lord.

There wasn't even a hint of a breeze when the disciples took to the sea without their Master. They didn't need Him. After all, many of them were experienced fishermen who knew the sea like the back of their hand. Before long, the scene had changed drastically. They were being tossed about by the strong wind and rising waves and fearfully they wondered if their time had come … and then Jesus got into the boat and everything calmed down. The wind and the sea as well as their fears were calmed. Jesus calms the storms in and around you.

Where is Jesus in your life? Did you leave Him
on the shore or is He with you in your lifeboat?

Lord Jesus, come and live in me and be part of my daily life. Amen.

March

The Courage to Believe

*"Every man must do two things alone;
he must do his own believing and his own dying."*

~ Martin Luther

*At the name of Jesus every knee should bow, in heaven and
on earth and under the earth, and every tongue acknowledge
that Jesus Christ is Lord, to the glory of God the Father.*

~ Philippians 2:10-11

Have Faith

The apostles said to the Lord, "Increase our faith!" (Luke 17:5)

We are all sometimes plagued by doubt. We have doubts about God, about the validity of the Gospel and we even doubt that He loves us. Sometimes we wonder when He will return like He promised He would. Or maybe you have been praying for a breakthrough for a very long time and it feels as if He doesn't hear you.

At other times, disaster strikes or we experience pain and disappointment and then we wonder if God is really there; if He knows how we are suffering … if He will deliver us.

If you pass through the valley of doubt from time to time, it doesn't mean that you have no faith. It certainly also doesn't mean that your Father will reject you for doubting. No, you are only human and humans sometimes have doubts.

God wants you to admit that you have doubts and He wants you to give your doubt and fear to Him. In times of a faith-crisis, pray that the Holy Spirit will plead on your behalf, will intercede for you and will lead you to the mountaintop of unshakable faith.

Holy Spirit, help me to have faith … when doubts threaten to overwhelm me. Amen.

Open Your Heart

For the message of the cross is foolishness to those who are perishing,
but to us who are being saved it is the power of God.
(1 Corinthians 1:18)

The Christian faith with its miraculous message of how God Himself came to this earth to save us, has through the years, been hard to swallow for many people.

But it really doesn't matter if others believe or not, the important question is: do you believe? Are you one hundred percent certain that Jesus was born as a baby, that He was God incarnate who came and lived among His people, that He died on the cross as our Savior and that He now reigns as the risen Lord? Or do you also sometimes have doubts?

There is only One who can convince you of this truth and that is the Holy Spirit. He is the One who refutes all the seemingly clever arguments of the world with the Truth. First Corinthians 1:19 reads as follows: "I will destroy the wisdom of the wise; the intelligence of the intelligent I will frustrate."

Today, open your heart and allow the Holy Spirit to impress on you that Jesus is the Son of God, that He died for you and that you are indeed saved by grace.

Thank You for being my God. Amen.

Say "Yes" to Jesus

"I told you that you would die in your sins; if you do not believe that I am He, you will indeed die in your sins." (John 8:24)

So how can we know for sure that Jesus really is the Son of God and that He came to save us? Jesus Himself gives us this assurance in John 5:36-39:

- Jesus performed numerous miracles. See what He says in verse 36: "I have testimony weightier than that of John. For the works that the Father has given Me to finish – the very works that I am doing – testify that the Father has sent Me."
- The second witness attesting to the fact that Jesus is the Messiah, is God the Father. When Jesus was baptized by John, God Himself said: "This is My Son, whom I love; with Him I am well pleased" (Matt. 3:17).
- The third thing that testifies to this is the Bible. In John 5:39, Jesus says, "These are the very Scriptures that testify about Me."

For you to be able to undertake your journey into eternity, you must put your faith in Jesus Christ. If you have accepted Him as your personal Lord and Savior, you have been saved and are a child of God. Give your heart to Him (again) today and then live your life with newfound joy.

Thank You, Father, for finding me and saving me through Your Son. Amen.

Growing Faith

"Very truly I tell you, the one who believes has eternal life. I am the bread of life." (John 6:47-48)

Karl Barth once said, "For our hearts to bear the fruit of the Holy Spirit, the seed of faith first needs to germinate in our hearts.

Has the seed of faith germinated in your heart? More specifically: are you convinced that Jesus Christ is your personal Savior and that He has truly redeemed you? Have you accepted His grace for you and do you live with enthusiasm because you know that you are His child? Do you have an authentic desire for a faith that is alive and fruitful?

Nobody can force you to believe. No one can make you believe. Only the Spirit of God can persuade you … if you allow Him to, that is. Today, ask the Spirit in particular to assure you of His love all the more every day. Also pray that He will let your mustard seed faith grow to become a massive tree of faith.

May your faith grow every day.

Spirit of God, thank You for creating passionate faith in me. Amen.

Believe without Reserve

For since in the wisdom of God the world through its wisdom did not know Him, God was pleased through the foolishness of what was preached to save those who believe. (1 Corinthians 1:21)

You believe that when you open the tap, water will come out; when you step on the gas, your car will accelerate; that the light will go on when you flip the switch and that the microwave will heat the milk.

We drive over bridges without first inspecting them, wholeheartedly convinced that they will not collapse under us. We only seem to have a problem with faith when it comes to God!

To have unshakable faith, you need to trust God with your whole heart. You need to take Him at His Word, accept that He is the Lord that can save you and live every day with the conviction that He can provide everything that you need in this life.

When you believe like a child, your life will change.
It will be easier, because you will have unreservedly
placed all your trust in the almighty God.

I live with the conviction that You are my God, Father! Amen.

Believe in God

They replied, "Believe in the Lord Jesus, and you will be saved – you and your household." (Acts 16:31)

There are two kinds of faith: first, a belief about God which means that I believe that what is said of God is true. This faith is rather a form of knowledge than a faith.

There is, secondly, faith in God which means that I put my trust in Him, give myself up to thinking that I can have dealings with Him, and believe without any doubt that He will be and do to me according to the things said of Him. Such faith, which throws itself upon God, whether in life or in death, alone makes a Christian.

How do you believe? Do you believe wholeheartedly in Christ, that He died for you and that He is your Savior? Does it excite you to know that He is the Living Lord who wants to call you His child and who loves you unconditionally?

Declare the following today: Great God, You are my Father, I know that Jesus died for me and I know that I am Your beloved child.

You truly are my personal Lord and Savior! Amen.

Touch His Wounds

Then He said to Thomas, "Put your finger here; see My hands. Reach out your hand and put it into My side. Stop doubting and believe." (John 20:27)

He was a close companion of Christ for three long years. He witnessed one miracle after another performed by Jesus, how the wind and the sea obeyed Him and how He changed people's lives.

He knew without a doubt that his Master was Lord and God. And yet, Thomas just couldn't get himself to believe that Jesus was resurrected from the dead … until Jesus Himself stood in front of him and invited him to put his hand into the wound in Jesus' side.

Wow, what an overwhelming moment it must have been for Thomas! His Lord really did rise from the grave. He is alive!

Dear friend, Jesus is also inviting you to look at the holes in His hands and to touch the wound in His side so that you can start each new day knowing: your Lord rose from the grave and lives … for your sake as well.

Thank You, Lord Jesus, for dying for me, and thank You most of all for living for me! Amen.

"My Lord and My God!"

Thomas said to Him, "My Lord and my God!" (John 20:28)

It must have been an incredible experience for the disciples to see their Friend and Confidante again after His death. Just think how overwhelmed we'll be on the day when Christ returns to come and take us to Him and tells us, "You are my beloved child."

Let's bow down before the Lord today and let's declare that He really is our Lord and our God. And then let's remember how Jesus responded to Thomas by saying, "Because you have seen Me, you have believed; blessed are those who have not seen and yet have believed" (John 20:29).

Today, see Jesus looking at you with nothing but love in His eyes. See the wounds in His hands and feel His arms around you in a compassionate embrace. Tell Him: "You are my Lord and my God!"

"God doesn't just give us grace, He gives us Jesus,
the Lord of grace," writes Joni Eareckson Tada. My cup
of joy overflows because of our Lord. How about yours?

I praise You for truly being my Lord and my God! Amen.

MARCH 9

Accept His Grace

This righteousness is given through faith in Jesus Christ to all who believe. (Romans 3:22)

One of the reasons why we sometimes struggle with our faith is that deep down inside we still believe that we need to earn God's grace. Life has taught us that we first need to give or perform, before we can receive anything. So we find it really hard to believe that God just gives His grace to those who least deserve it; to those who, however, need it most: sinners.

God's gift of grace is free and is given to people like you and me, people who struggle to do the right thing and whose lives are, more often than not, quite a mess. But our Lord's grace cannot be earned, it can only be received and accepted with a thankful heart.

Remember that grace is not a verb. In fact, it implies no action at all. Christ already did everything that needed to be done and it cost Him His life! For that reason, you can rest in the knowledge that you don't have to do a thing and it won't cost you anything either.

You either receive God's grace for free, or you don't at all. Today, make sure you receive the free gift.

Thank You, Lord, that I know that it is through grace that I have been saved and that I can live with joy because of it. Amen.

Accept the Free Gift

Where, then, is boasting? It is excluded. Because of what law? The law that requires works? No, because of the law that requires faith. (Romans 3:27)

Women are often under the illusion that they must always do something. Because if we do nothing, we are apparently lazy or good for nothing. That's pure nonsense! Particularly when it comes to faith.

Philip Yancey writes: "Grace means there is nothing we can do to make God love us more. And grace means there is nothing we can do to make God love us less. Grace means that God loves us as much as an infinite God can possibly love."

"For we maintain that a person is justified by faith apart from the works of the law" (Rom. 3:28). What a joy to know that we don't need to prove ourselves to God before He saves us.

Grace says, "Relax, my child. I have already
done everything that was needed." Accept this
divine gift of grace today, without feeling like you
need to do something in return. Now that's faith!

Savior, thank You for doing everything that needed to be done. Amen.

Live without Guilt

For all have sinned and fall short of the glory of God, and all are justified freely by His grace through the redemption that came by Christ Jesus. God presented Christ as a sacrifice of atonement, through the shedding of His blood – to be received by faith. (Romans 3:23-25)

Women make lists. Apart from the grocery list, every new day comes with its own infinitely long to-do list. And when we page through a magazine, we find yet more lists, this time a ten-steps-to-a-new-you list or something of the sort. No wonder you find it hard to accept the fact that God does not expect you to work through a checklist before you can be His child.

On top of that, our hearts and lives are so full of cracks that we struggle to accept His healing love just like that. The fact of the matter is: God has declared us righteous. Not because we did something right or because we will do something right or because our lives are all in order.

No, it is as Paul writes, because God loves us. Our wrong deeds no longer count against us when we put our faith in Him (Rom. 3:25).

Make His grace your own today. Accept it
and then go and live your life – without
shame and guilt – as a joyful child of God!

Thank You, Lamb of God, that You have freed me and that I can now live without guilt and shame. Amen.

"Here I Stand"

For in the gospel the righteousness of God is revealed – a righteousness that is by faith from first to last, just as it is written: "The righteous will live by faith." (Romans 1:17)

In 1999, Martin Luther was appointed the third most influential person of the previous millennium, and with good reason. His words of reformation uttered in 1521 shook the foundations of the church of those days: "Here I stand, I can do no other, so help me God."

Luther had the courage to protest against the rigid religion-of-good-deeds that was only available to the elect. After spending years and years intensely studying the Bible and even grappling with God, he came to the conclusion that filled him with gratitude. God's grace was sufficient for him. As well as for every single sinner on earth.

By coming to this insight, he placed God and His Word back into the hearts and lives of ordinary people – people like you and me.

Faith is to say to God, "Lord, here I stand.
Just as I am." Grace is when the Lord responds,
"I have already paid the price. I have ransomed
you, My child. You are Mine. Just as you are."

Thank You, my Savior, that I can find rest in Your arms … just as I am. Amen.

"Lord, Save Me!"

Then Peter got down out of the boat, walked on the water and came toward Jesus. But when he saw the wind, he was afraid and, beginning to sink, cried out, "Lord, save me!" (Matthew 14:29-30)

It must have been a wonderful experience for Peter to get out of the boat and to be able to walk on the water toward Jesus. How great and powerful is the Lord! And then?

Then he shifted his gaze away from his Master and he saw the overwhelmingly high waves. He became fraught with fear and started sinking. He then cried out, "Lord, save me!" And even before he went under, Jesus was there, grabbed his hand and saved him.

That same Lord Jesus is still standing at the ready today. He is willing and able to carry you through any situation, to hold you when things seem overwhelming and to keep you safe amid the storms of life.

Today, don't look at the storm, but direct your
gaze at Jesus who is ready to take your hand.
Just say, "Lord, help me!" He will!

Master, I am too weak. Please help me, save me! Amen.

Keep Believing

Now faith is confidence in what we hope for and assurance about what we do not see. (Hebrews 11:1)

Sometimes, especially in times that you need God the most, it may feel like you don't hear from Him. You pray and it doesn't work; you ask Him for the solution, but He doesn't answer you; you plead for something that He just doesn't give you.

It is in such times that we need to persevere in our faith. These are the times when you should not stop calling out to Him; but keep searching for answers in His Word guided by the Spirit. Trust Him blindly.

That is when you need to declare what was found written on a cellar wall during the holocaust: "I believe in the sun even when it's not shining; I believe in love even when I can't feel it; I believe in God even when He is silent."

If you still see His light in overcast times, if you keep declaring your love for God in times when you are down and if you stay faithful in days that leave you speechless ... then you truly believe. When you have faith like that, He will give you hope. Eternal hope.

Lord, I know that You are with me – now and always. Amen.

MARCH 15

Rely on His Care

So if you faithfully obey the commands I am giving you today – to love the LORD your God and to serve Him with all your heart and with all your soul – then I will send rain on your land in its season, both autumn and spring rains, so that you may gather in your grain, new wine and olive oil. I will provide grass in the fields for your cattle, and you will eat and be satisfied. (Deuteronomy 11:13-15)

Sometimes when we think of the future, we feel anxious. We can ask the same question concerning tomorrow a thousand times over: "What if … ?"

Faith indeed means that we must put our trust in God to be saved and to have eternal life. Our Father, however, also wants us to trust Him with the little things, the everyday things. And you should!

During tough times in your life, hold on to Him, knowing that He will send the rain at the right time. When your heart feels like it is going to freeze over because the world is so cold and bitter, pray and ask Him to cover you with His cozy blanket of mercy.

God has always taken care of His children. So, you can live your life knowing that when you do your part, your caring Father will fill your bread basket with His provision.

Thank You, Lord, that I know that You will take care of me. Amen.

To Leave It in His Hands

I will restore their fortunes and have compassion on them.
(Jeremiah 33:26)

Are you also one of those people who want to lend God a hand? Are you so used to always being in control of everything that you think God needs your help? As a result, you exhaust yourself trying to make things run smoothly as well as better and faster. You constantly worry about tomorrow and spend nights tossing and turning, trying to find a solution for your problems.

Stormie Omartian says, "There have been so many times in my life when I've worn myself out trying to help God get me to where I thought I should be … But the more I learned to praise the all-powerful God of the universe, the more I could sense His power working in my life."

Don't you want to leave things up to your Father more often?

Thank You that I can rest knowing that I really don't have to help You. You are God! And You are my Father. Amen.

Look Back

You may say to yourselves, "These nations are stronger than we are. How can we drive them out?" But do not be afraid of them; remember well what the LORD your God did to Pharaoh and to all Egypt. You saw with your own eyes the great trials, the signs and wonders, the mighty hand and outstretched arm, with which the LORD your God brought you out. The LORD your God will do the same to all the peoples you now fear. (Deuteronomy 7:17-19)

There are times when our faith is in full bloom, and then there are days when our faith seems to wither: when we doubt that He loves us, when we struggle to trust Him completely, when we feel like we can't connect with Him.

It is important to look back in such times, to remember how wonderful it was when He lead you out of sin's captivity, how He stayed faithfully by your side, guiding you through all those seasons in the wilderness. Think back on the times when you didn't know which way to turn and He showed you the way; or the days when you called out to Him for help and He sent manna and quails or when you unexpectedly stumbled on a fountain of living water.

Remember how He spoilt you, His child.

Look back on your journey of faith often and be reminded of how wonderfully faithful God is. Let it strengthen your faith!

Thank You for being my Guide, in the past, now and always. Amen.

Expect Good Things

Out of His fullness we have all received grace in place of grace already given. (John 1:16)

Whenever people get together, they tend to complain. It is just so easy to bemoan our lot in life, to get upset about something and to see only the dark side of things.

Throughout the years, not much has changed. In Numbers 11 we read how the Israelites kept complaining and longing to return to Egypt, despite the fact that God took care of them in a miraculous way in the desert.

Complaining is actually like a big "motion of no confidence" in God's goodness. When we complain, we communicate that we don't trust God completely, because we want something else … something more. While we actually have more than enough and that is reason enough to be grateful.

> God wants only the very best for you. Make an effort
> today to spot all the drops of grace with which
> God showers you and then be courageous enough
> to be a nothing-to-complain-about person.

Thank You, Father of my life, for all the goodness flowing forth from Your hand. Amen.

Really See the Quail

*Now a wind went out from the LORD and drove quail in from the sea.
It scattered them up to two cubits deep all around the camp, as far
as a day's walk in any direction. (Numbers 11:31)*

All of us go through times when we see, but can't seem to perceive
God's grace – just like the Israelites so many years ago. In these times,
we usually either try to survive on our own or we focus on the world
and then forget all about God.

We compare ourselves to others and wish we had more. Yes, we all
feel unhappy with our lives at times, even though we really have nothing to complain about.

History has proven that God always takes care of His children and
that He will provide what they need at exactly the right time. The
problem lies with us, however, because we often want a lot more than
what we need. And that makes us dissatisfied, greedy and disgruntled.

Today, focus on all the quail-of-grace that God's wind
blows your way. Thank and praise Him for it, knowing
that you can trust Him to provide everything you need.

*Please forgive me for being unhappy with what I have, Lord, and help
me to really perceive Your grace in my life. Amen.*

Live Out Your Faith

"A new command I give you: Love one another. As I have loved you, so you must love one another. By this everyone will know that you are My disciples, if you love one another." (John 13:34-35)

Where is your faith? Is it deeply buried under the worldly way of living that you acquired over the years? Or is it out there in the open for all to see, hear and experience?

Ask yourself today, "Do I look just like everyone else or can other people sense who my Lord is? Does the way I live offer sufficient proof of the fact that I am a child of the God of love?"

Hidden faith will not convince anyone. When your heart is full of God's love, you cannot help but make it evident for all to see. Then you just want to share the love and peace He placed in your heart with others. Then your faith will become evident in your words and deeds.

Pray that every person who comes your way today
will see something of your Father's great grace,
goodness and love in you. God immeasurably blesses
His children who stand out because of their faith.

Spirit of God, show me how to live out my faith in a way that is visible, audible and tangible. Amen.

Remain in His Light

Anyone who loves their brother and sister lives in the light, and there is nothing in them to make them stumble. (1 John 2:10)

I am amazed at how we, committed believers, can still veer off course at times. We feel far-removed from God when we are in conflict with someone else or when there is something that causes trouble in our relationship. It is almost as if a troubled relationship causes gaps in your connection with God.

There is only one way to keep living in peace with ourselves, those around us and our Father and that is to be filled with His peace every morning. His Light is there to help us to get rid of strife in our relationships, to drive the darkness out of our hearts and to get us back on the right track. When you feel far away from God, pray and ask His Spirit to remove from your heart whatever causes you to stumble so that you can see the Light again.

Do not allow anything or any relationship to encumber your faith. Make things right and make things whole today.

Please let Your light shine on us today so that we can live in peace. Amen.

Use Your Faith

The apostles said to the Lord, "Increase our faith!" (Luke 17:5)

Do you sometimes feel like giving up? Do you think: "I will never be able to do everything that God expects of me"?

I think every single child of God feels like this from time to time. Like the disciples, we want to say, "Lord, it is so hard to do all these things You say and we have so little faith." When you occasionally doubt your faith abilities, just remember how Jesus responded to His friends. He said, "If you have faith as small as a mustard seed, you can say to this mulberry tree, 'Be uprooted and planted in the sea,' and it will obey you" (Luke 17:6). A little faith is more than enough so use what you have!

> Dear fellow believer, do not doubt your faith.
> Do not give up. Just try to stay strong in the faith
> every day, to do what He asks of you and make sure
> to use the (little or much) faith that you have!

Father, thank You that I know that You can do great things with my little faith, because You are great. Amen.

Mature in the Faith

He replied, "If you have faith as small as a mustard seed, you can say to this mulberry tree, 'Be uprooted and planted in the sea,' and it will obey you." (Luke 17:6)

God knows us through and through. He knows exactly how fragile our human faith is. He watches over us as we keep stumbling around in our baby shoes of faith and notices when we trip over sin and doubt. And then He feels sorry for us. He wants to help us.

God really does want to see us grow up and move from our toddler-in-the-faith phase to a joyful mature-in-the-faith phase. He wants us to become mature so that He can feed us solid food.

Growing your faith is a never-ending process. You have to declare your dependence on your Father anew every day. You have to seek His will with new zeal, delve into His Word continually and pray for the Holy Spirit to keep working in your heart. If you have a genuine desire to mature in the faith, then you have to work at it to make it happen.

Pray and ask the Holy Spirit to make you more devoted, more enthusiastic and stronger in the faith every day.

Dearest Father, I really want more faith. Make me a willing learner at Your service. Amen.

He Is Everywhere

"I am the good shepherd; I know My sheep and My sheep know Me."
(John 10:14)

Being a believer does not mean that nothing bad will ever happen to you. No, there will always be some things in life that will make us unhappy, hurt us, disappoint us or leave us feeling that life is unfair.

But, the life of a child of God is different! We have the assurance that we don't have to handle anything in life alone. Because God is with us always and in all circumstances. Even in times of discomfort, rejection and sadness when we feel alone and as if God has abandoned us … He is still there.

Hear Jesus' own words as He says, "I lay down My life for the sheep" (John 10:15). How wonderful it is to know that your God is always on your side.

Take Him along ... everywhere you go and experience
how His presence changes the outcome.

Thank You for being my Companion in every situation and everywhere.
Amen.

Make Your Faith Work

The warden paid no attention to anything under Joseph's care, because the LORD was with Joseph and gave him success in whatever he did. (Genesis 39:23)

Those who have faith do things differently. Abraham, for instance, packed up and moved to an unknown destination. He believed that he would be a father even though he was a hundred years old and later he went to sacrifice his only son in obedience to God's command.

Joseph trusted God blindly while he was in the pit and in the jail cell and in the end, he became king. Moses lead the people through the wilderness to Canaan because he had faith. Similarly, Gideon, Barak, Samson and Jephthah, David and Samuel and many others managed the impossible … because they trusted God and had faith. Trusting God transforms an ordinary life into a wonderful adventure.

What is the effect of your faith? It is making a difference to your life and to the lives of the people around you?

May your faith be so strong that God's glorious power will flow through you into every area of your life. May He, through the power of your faith, make the impossible possible.

Make my life an adventure lived by faith so that others can see You in it. Amen.

Have Faith in Your Prayers

"Before they call I will answer; while they are still speaking I will hear."
(Isaiah 65:24)

Do you really believe that what you pray for, will come to pass? That God can make the impossible possible and that your prayers can make a difference in your life? Or do you pray without hope? God did not give us the ability to pray for no reason. He doesn't only want us to share our thoughts with Him, but He also wants to hear our requests and petitions … so that He can answer our prayers – according to His will.

Andrew Murray said that prayer is absolutely necessary for everything that God wants to establish in this world. Prayer combined with faith is very powerful. Even more than that: your prayers can change your life as well as the lives of other people completely, because prayer has great power!

Pray every prayer in faith with the conviction
that God can and will answer it, if He thinks
that it will be in your best interests.

Thank You, Father, for answering even before I asked. Please help me to pray and have faith. Amen.

Be His Voice

[May He] encourage your hearts and strengthen you in every good deed and word. (2 Thessalonians 2:17)

It is impossible to believe in God wholeheartedly … and then to keep silent about Him. Just like a young person in love cannot keep themselves from talking about their beloved, we can also not be silent about how great and good our God is. The closer you get to God, the more you become aware of His gracious love and the easier it becomes to spontaneously talk about Him.

May your faith be so strong that you can easily and comfortably tell others how great your God is. May you experience His love for you so intensely that it spontaneously overflows and causes you to love others in the same way. Yes, may you experience His Spirit speaking through you every day of your life, because you want to be His voice.

When you are willing to witness for Him,
you will see that He will say the right things
at the right time through you.

Lord, I want to be an instrument that You can use. Amen.

Stand Your Ground

But the Lord is faithful, and He will strengthen you and protect you from the evil one. (2 Thessalonians 3:3)

Satan and his demons are a reality. Especially in the lives of believers. The devil will do everything in his power to make you doubt, to steal your faith and to encourage you to sin.

Thomas Watson said, "Sin has the devil for its father, shame for its companion, and death for its wages." And therefore, the Word warns us in Ephesians 6:11-12: "Put on the full armor of God, so that you can take your stand against the devil's schemes. For our struggle is not against flesh and blood, but against the rulers, against the authorities, against the powers of this dark world and against the spiritual forces of evil in the heavenly realms."

Dear believer, arm yourself against every attack every day. Pray that the Spirit will protect you and strengthen you to endure every attack. Know that when God is on your side, the devil is powerless.

Stand your ground! Have faith, pray continually and know that God has already defeated the Evil One.

Protect me, my family and every other believer against Your enemies, please Father. Amen.

Put on the Full Armor of God

Finally, be strong in the Lord and in His mighty power.
(Ephesians 6:10)

God gave His children protective gear. So, let's put on the outfit as described by Paul in Ephesians 6:13-18 every day.

Buckle truth around your waist like a belt. The knowledge that God declared you righteous must protect your chest like an iron breastplate. You must always wear the readiness to tell other people about the peace that Jesus gives like shoes on your feet. Then there is your faith. Use your intimate relationship with the Lord like a shield with which you can ward off the vicious attacks of the Evil One.

You are no longer bound by sin. No, you have been saved. That assurance is like an iron helmet that protects your face and head.

God's message, His Word, is like a sword that
the Holy Spirit gives you so that you can prevail
in battle. It doesn't matter what happens, always
keep praying and stay dressed in the armor of faith.

Thank You for equipping me to be strong, Holy Spirit. Amen.

Believe in Miracles

Peter sent them all out of the room; then he got down on his knees and prayed. Turning toward the dead woman, he said, "Tabitha, get up." She opened her eyes, and seeing Peter she sat up. (Acts 9:40)

Tabitha was a very special, caring person. So, her friends were heart-broken when she passed away. But then we read how the Spirit enabled Peter to resurrect her from the dead. What an amazing miracle!

We serve a God of miracles – a God who still does many, seen and unseen, miracles in people's lives every day. Sometimes the miracle grabs your attention because it is a big occurrence and sometimes the miracle is a quiet, and yet dramatic, change in someone's heart.

Too often we attribute these divine interventions to mere coincidence or some or other unexplainable event and we do that because we no longer really believe that our Lord still does miracles in this day and age.

Open your eyes and ears and take note of every
big and small miracle that God does in your life.
There may be a lot more than you think.

Help me, Father, to remember that with You, nothing is impossible. Open my eyes and ears so that I can truly experience Your greatness. Amen.

To Expect Your Own Canaan

In spite of this, you did not trust in the LORD your God, who went ahead of you on your journey, in fire by night and in a cloud by day, to search out places for you to camp and to show you the way you should go. (Deuteronomy 1:32-33)

God has a Promised Land in store for all of us: a place of milk and honey where we will always be happy. Sometimes, however, we allow the world's problems to get us down and then we start feeling hopeless and we lose sight of where we're headed. Just like the Israelites of old, our focus is on the circumstances and the people around us and so we don't see how great and mighty our God is.

Remember, God is greater and mightier than all your problems. So, you can trust Him with every step of your life's journey. Yes. Even when you feel overwhelmed. Therefore, look for God's grace in everything and remember that He will faithfully lead you … until you stand in front of His throne one day.

God will let you enter into your Promised Land. Just trust Him.

Dear Lord, I want to trust You completely. Thank You that I know I can. Thank You that I also know that You will never leave me. Amen.

April

The Courage to Be like Him

*"We must always change, renew,
rejuvenate ourselves; otherwise, we harden."*

~ Johann Wolfgang von Goethe

*[We are all] being transformed into His image with ever-increasing
glory, which comes from the Lord, who is the Spirit.*

~ 2 Corinthians 3:18

Live Every Day Anew

[The Holy Spirit], whom He poured out on us generously through Jesus Christ our Savior. (Titus 3:6)

God loves you more than you would ever know. He loves you so much that even if you were the only person on earth, He would still have given His life for you – just you! And this great gift of grace is new every morning. It doesn't matter where you were yesterday, what you did or didn't do. God's mercies for you are brand new every morning.

Take a moment to contemplate this and allow the Holy Spirit to let you become aware of His unconditional, merciful love for you once again.

Come to the realization of how great, comprehensive and new His love is for you – for the person that you are. Today, receive His complete forgiveness, His saving grace and redemptive love for you.

Every morning, God starts over with us. So, go
down on your knees again before the God that loves
you with His life and thank Him for everything.

Thank You, Jesus, Thank You! Thank You for cleansing, redeeming and saving me! Amen.

Focus on Him

Let us run with perseverance the race marked out for us, fixing our eyes on Jesus ... (Hebrews 12:1-2)

Not all of us are built for athletics. And yet, as believers, we all have to run our life race every day while a crowd of believers who lived before us, keep an eye on us. Wow, just think about it for a moment; great men like Moses, Abraham, Gideon, David, Samuel and Paul are sitting on the pavilion of our lives, watching and encouraging us every day. They're probably saying things like: "Well done, faithful participant. Keep going!"

As encouragement, Paul writes the following in Hebrews 12:1-2: "Therefore, since we are surrounded by such a great cloud of witnesses, let us throw off everything that hinders and the sin that so easily entangles. And let us run with perseverance the race marked out for us, fixing our eyes on Jesus, the pioneer and perfecter of faith."

Dear friend-in-Christ, I know the race of life
is not always easy. So, let's pray that we will all
have the courage, the strength and the perseverance
to stay faithful and to keep focusing on Him.

Help me to focus on You, Lord Jesus, so that I can keep going with confidence. Amen.

Follow His Example

For the joy set before Him, He [Jesus] endured the cross, scorning its
shame, and sat down at the right hand of the throne of God.
(Hebrews 12:2)

To start every morning full of courage takes a whole lot of self-discipline,
positive thinking, perseverance and faith. Our days are not always filled
with sunshine; we all have days when we just feel really tired, hopeless,
upset and worried. It's usually in times like these, that our faith seems
to become diluted … and then we feel even worse.

So today, think of the path that Jesus walked for your sake. He did
not hesitate for a single moment on the *Via Dolorosa*, because He
knew: He was doing it for every believer who has the courage to follow
Him. He was doing it so that you and I can one day be with Him and
experience indescribable joy and peace.

Let's follow our Lord's example to always stay faithful
to our Father in all circumstances. We can do this,
because we know that His grace goes before us.

Lord Jesus, please give me the courage to really persevere, just like You
did. Amen.

Be an Advertisement for Christ

Whatever happens, conduct yourselves in a manner worthy of the gospel of Christ. (Philippians 1:27)

Imagine your life was a massive billboard next to the highway. What if a women's magazine published an article on your life every month? What do you think it would say? What would people read?

The fact of the matter is, as people who know Christ, we are living advertisements of His love every day. A lot of people don't read the Bible. But, they see how you live! They look at your life in order to decide if it is worth it to be a Christ follower.

Now we all know that there are two kinds of advertisements. The one that persuades you at once and then you take action to get hold of the product. The other one is less remarkable. It doesn't make a lasting impression on you, so it gets lost among all the thousands of other advertisements. What is your life-advertisement like? Does it grab other people's attention? Will it persuade them to take action to become a Christ follower like you?

Pray today and ask the Spirit to direct your life in such a way that others will want to get to know your Lord Jesus.

Redesign me, please. Change me so that I can really look like You, Jesus. Amen.

Live in His Spotlight

"He must become greater; I must become less!" (John 3:30)

Our lives here on earth can be compared to a play. Every day, we perform an act or two on the stage-of-life while the world is our audience. Sometimes, we get a standing ovation, sometimes there is nothing but an uncomfortable silence and at other times, we get booed off stage.

To be a successful Christ actor, we need to do only one thing: we must become less so that the image of Christ can become more and more. Because the more I substitute myself and my own will with Him, the greater role I will play in the Kingdom of God. It may mean that the world will not applaud me as much anymore and that I could even get the cold shoulder at times. But one thing is certain: when I allow Christ to speak and act through me, I will deliver a performance that will fill the heavenly audience with awe.

Let Paul motivate you today with what he writes
in Hebrews 12:3: "Consider Him [Jesus] who
endured such opposition from sinners, so that
you will not grow weary and lose heart."

Lord Jesus, please become more so that I can become less. Yes, Lord, let me live to glorify only You. Amen.

Perform for Heaven

But whenever anyone turns to the Lord, the veil is taken away. Now the Lord is the Spirit, and where the Spirit of the Lord is, there is freedom. And we all, who with unveiled faces contemplate the Lord's glory, are being transformed into His image with ever-increasing glory. (2 Corinthians 3:16-18)

We often wonder what others think of us and how we can make them happy. Yes, we all sometimes perform for the worldly audience in the hope of getting a little recognition. This, however, also means that we often deliver performances with which God is not happy at all.

Francis Bacon once said, "But men must know, that in this theater of man's life it is reserved only for God and angels to be lookers on."

When we shift our focus and strive to do God's will, our lives change dramatically. It is then that the curtains of the heavenly stage open so that people can see God's glory in us.

> When you perform for the heavenly audience,
> you will also deliver an excellent earthly
> performance. Because you will be showing
> the world something of God's amazing love.

Lord Jesus, help me to live my life in such a way that it elicits an applause from You and Your angels. Amen.

Live Out His Goodness

But whoever does not have them is nearsighted and blind, forgetting that they have been cleansed from their past sins. (2 Peter 1:9)

Sometimes I am stunned by humanity! The injustice we do one another, the damage we cause to other people's lives and the way we hurt one another … I then can't help but wonder how our dear Father remains patient with us!

In times when we are faced with such terrible things, we need to remember how Jesus acted towards the evil in this world. We need to remind ourselves that He is the one Person who overcame all the sin in this world once and for all and, therefore, good will one day triumph over evil.

We need to keep praying that His glory will fill the earth, that His Kingdom will come and that His love will change people's hearts.

You and I can make a difference in this world
if we express Jesus' kindness towards other people
through the way we live; by noticing and responding
to other's needs, by reaching out and by caring.

Savior God, please show me where, how and to whom I can show Your kindness today. Amen.

You Are Set Free

But now that you have been set free from sin and have become slaves of God, the benefit you reap leads to holiness, and the result is eternal life. (Romans 6:22)

After yesterday's devotion you may feel a little skeptical about the fact that you – being only one person – can make a difference in this big world. Well, if all of us doubted that we could have an influence on the world around us, none of us would have any impact.

The wonderful thing, however, is that God does not need scores of people. He uses only one person to work in many people's lives. When you and I willingly follow Him, when we strive to live out His example, we can leave the impact we make up to Him. The Holy Spirit has a way of performing miracles through only one willing person.

Dear friend, you really can make a difference in your family, at your workplace, in your community and in every other social circle that you're a part of. You can change other people's lives completely through the way you think, speak and act, because they will see Christ's merciful love and kindness in you.

Go and show the people around you
just how great your God's love is today.

Help me, Lamb of God, to emulate You. Amen.

Safe in His Hands

You show that you are a letter from Christ, the result of our ministry, written not with ink but with the Spirit of the living God, not on tablets of stone but on tablets of human hearts. (2 Corinthians 3:3)

Maybe you feel like I do sometimes – that is, utterly incompetent and unable to be a worthy representative of the holy Lord here on earth. After all, we all know how fallible we are. God, however, never sends His children into the world unprepared. He gives us His very own Spirit to rejuvenate us every day, to carry us and to help us bear His image on earth.

So, know this today: your Father will never leave you. Especially if your greatest desire is to do His will. If you place your life in His hands, He will write every second of your life with the ink of His grace.

Live today being fully convinced of the fact
that you can do all things through Him.

Lord, thank You for making me new, strong and ... more Christlike every day. Amen.

See His Light

This is the message we have heard from Him and declare to you: God is light; in Him there is no darkness at all. (1 John 1:5)

God is light. Everything about Him is light, everything He does and everything that He is, is pure, bright light. The light that brings about beauty, that radiates love and that results in perfection. That is light that gives life.

When God's light is present somewhere, when it shines in someone's heart, it dispels every last little bit of darkness. Whatever is evil or bad, literally flees when God's light approaches. When we desire to do God's will and to follow the Holy Spirit's lead, we become part of His glorious glow. Because He is in us, we are the rays that light up this world with faith, hope and love. Allow His light to fill you from corner to corner every day. Ask Him to light up every dark corner in your heart and pray that you will be a carrier of His bright light.

Let the Holy Spirit shine through you today!

Holy Spirit, please remove every dark spot from my life and replace it with Your heavenly light of peace. Amen.

More like Him

If we claim to have fellowship with Him and yet walk in the darkness, we lie and do not live out the truth. But if we walk in the light, as He is in the light, we have fellowship with one another, and the blood of Jesus, His Son, purifies us from all sin. (1 John 1:6-7)

Do you think that the people who you know can see that you are related to God? Would you say that you live in the light? Does your life show that you love your Brother, Jesus, with all your heart and can others see that you really want to be like Him?

These are not easy questions and they make us feel uncomfortable! Very few of us are able to live our lives in such a way that our Master's light shines from us.

Dear fellow believer, don't feel discouraged. God knows your heart, He knows how much you love Him and how you desire to glorify Him with your life. Fortunately, He also knows our human weaknesses and He wants to help us overcome them.

Pray and ask the Holy Spirit to remove every lie that has taken root in your heart so that the Truth can become visible in the way you live. He wants to help you with this and He will do it. After all, He is your beloved Brother.

Lord, will You make me like You, please? Amen.

APRIL 12

Live in His Light

Anyone who loves their brother and sister lives in the light, and there is nothing in them to make them stumble. But anyone who hates a brother or sister is in the darkness and walks around in the darkness. They do not know where they are going, because the darkness has blinded them. (1 John 2:10-11)

John touches on a question that remains relevant even today, centuries later: how does one distinguish a person who lives in the light from one who doesn't? The answer he provides (above) is just as relevant.

God's light simply cannot be hidden. It is just too powerful and holy. And there are many ways to live out His light; by caring, by showing genuine interest in other people's lives, by valuing others and helping them. It all speaks volumes. In addition, people can see God's light in His children in so many ways as well. They see the compassion, understanding and love in their eyes and in the way that they give of themselves. People can also hear it in their words; what God's children say as well as the love with which they say it.

You can feel God's love when you're around children of the light, because where they are, He is and where He is, is heavenly sunlight.

Do other people see, hear and feel Him when they are around you?

Father, make Your light of truth so much a part of my life that the world can see You in me every day. Amen.

The Courage to Repent

But if we walk in the light, as He is in the light, we have fellowship with one another, and the blood of Jesus, His Son, purifies us from all sin. (1 John 1:7)

It doesn't matter how much of a believer you are or how hard you try to walk in His light, we all make mistakes that make us feel ashamed. And then Satan is right there to make us feel even worse, like we are not even worthy to be called God's children, let alone to be of any kind of service to Him!

God knows us. So, He also knows that – despite all our best efforts – we will never be without fault, sin or darkness. And that is exactly why He sent His own Light to the world to pay for our weaknesses. How fortunate are we that there was Someone willing to take all our sin on Himself!

Don't run away from God when you feel guilty for failing.
Confess your sin and then know that He has forgiven you.
Then turn back to the Light and live victoriously.

Thank You, Lord Jesus, for forgiving me time after time. Amen.

Become Strong

If we confess our sins, He is faithful and just and will forgive us our sins and purify us from all unrighteousness. (1 John 1:9)

We all have our weaknesses – things that we just can't seem to overcome no matter how much we want to or how hard we try. Bad habits, shortcomings that encumber us and pet sins that we just don't want to let go of. We pray about these things for years on end and try to overcome them, but we just can't seem to succeed.

When you genuinely desire to be Christlike, His Spirit will enable you to do anything. His Word promises to help us, especially when we are weak, and to give us the courage we need to be victorious.

Believe today that you really can overcome any challenging sin, that you will rise above even the darkest times of weakness and that He will always pick you up again – even when you feel defeated.

Thank You for never leaving me; and that You are strong. Make me strong when I am weak. Amen.

Let His Love Bloom

But if anyone obeys His word, love for God is truly made complete in them. This is how we know we are in Him: Whoever claims to live in Him must live as Jesus did. (1 John 2:5-6)

Flowers always touch a woman's heart. It doesn't matter if it is red roses from a lover, a bouquet of bright flowers from a friend or even a single daisy from your toddler. Flowers make a woman bloom because they convey a message of adoration and love.

You and I are God's flowers here on earth. We are here to change people's hearts with our love. Sometimes the love we give is in the form of a big bouquet of brightly colored acts of love that impress others. And other times, our love is simply lily white and given anonymously. And then there are those times that we completely change someone else's life with a simple, yet profound, daisy-act-of-love.

The kind of love flowers you give or how they are delivered doesn't matter. It always makes a difference to the receiver's life. So, be generous and give flowers today!

Son of God, show me how to be Your florist today. Amen.

APRIL 16

Hear Again

[Jesus] got up, rebuked the wind and said to the waves, "Quiet! Be still!" Then the wind died down and it was completely calm.
(Mark 4:39)

Are there certain sounds that bring back special memories for you? Like your mother's caring voice filled with love, the cheerful sounds of the ice-cream truck, songs that make you miss someone or even the familiar babbling of your children when they were young?

Sounds stir up emotions. The question is: Do you still hear them? Or have you grown a little deaf due to the everyday noise of life? So deaf that you no longer hear the beautiful sounds. That you no longer really hear your beloved's words. That you no longer hear God's voice.

Today, make an effort to really listen and hear again. But more than that, take some time and listen to what God wants to say to you, "I am in control. You can be still. Be calm."

The Spirit speaks to us even through the noise
of life, but when you are calm and quiet, His voice
is a thousand times clearer. Can you hear Him?

Great Creator, please open my heart and ears so that I can once again hear the wonderful sounds of life. Amen.

Feel with Your Heart

We are therefore Christ's ambassadors, as though God were making His appeal through us. (2 Corinthians 5:20)

Jesus was passionate about people. That is why He spontaneously touched them, comforted them and held them in His arms and His heart.

We see the following in the Bible:

- When Jesus saw the woman that had been crippled by a spirit for years, He felt sorry for her (Luke 13:12).
- When Jesus' disciples wanted to keep the children away from Him, Jesus rebuked them for it and we see in Mark 10:16 that "He took the children in His arms, placed His hands on them and blessed them."
- Two blind men begged Jesus to help them, we read in Matthew 20:34 that "Jesus had compassion on them and touched their eyes. Immediately they received their sight and followed Him."

Do you also have a passionate love for other people? Can they feel it in your touch and do they see it in your eyes?

Live out Jesus' love wholeheartedly today.

Lord, give me a heart filled with empathy, understanding and love for others. Amen.

Serve Others

"The Son of Man did not come to be served, but to serve, and to give His life as a ransom for many." (Matthew 20:28)

If Jesus had come to earth to impose His will on others and to make all kinds of demands because He is the King, this world would have been a horrible place. Because if He was only interested in sitting on the throne and displaying His power, He would never have been willing to die on the cross for us!

So today, let's just thank our Lord Jesus because He is so great that He – the King – came to show us how to wash each other's feet and how to sacrifice ourselves for others. In His greatness, He came and set a clear example of how to really serve other people.

Do you and I really serve? Do we really express enough of Jesus' love? Or do we just sit on our little self-made thrones?

Master, please give me a heart that is willing to serve. A life that is an expression of a humble servant heart. Amen.

Live Out the Truth

[Diotrephes is] spreading malicious nonsense about us. (3 John 1:10)

Have you ever been in a position where other people spread rumors and lies about you? And then you found out that they had talked about you behind your back?

John found himself in this position when Diotrephes – a prominent member of the church in Ephesus – spread all kinds of lies about him. That is why John asks Gaius for help in his third letter. John wanted the church to know the truth.

The fact of the matter is that the truth will always come out. Our faithful Father will let the lie come to light sooner or later. Yes, He is cooperating with the righteous to ensure that the truth triumphs over the lie. So, in times when you feel like evil is prevailing over good, you should just put all your trust in God. He is capable of ensuring that honor and justice always prevail.

Make sure that you are always on the side of the truth,
in all circumstances. Because that is the side that will win!

Thank You, Lord, for being the God of Truth. Keep me from ever being a child of lies. Amen.

APRIL 20

Be His Display Window

*It gave me great joy when some believers came and testified about
your faithfulness to the truth, telling how you continue to walk in it.
(3 John 1:3)*

When people have disappointed us, talked about us behind our back
and let us down, it is really hard to trust them again. The good news,
however, is that not everyone in life is devious, backstabbing and blind
to the truth. There will always be people who you can rely on because
they are loyal and honest.

In the passage above, it is clear that John was happy that Gaius
was indeed living out the truth – unlike Diotrephes. In fact, John even
compares Gaius's way of living to a "display window for the truth".

Maybe we should ask ourselves the following question: Am I – in
terms of my thoughts, words and actions – a display window for the
truth? If you are honest and can answer "yes" to this question, then at
least you are someone whom other people can trust.

Make this world a better place by displaying His truth in your life.

Jesus, I want to live out Your truth! Amen.

Follow His Pattern

Dear friend [Gaius], do not imitate what is evil but what is good. Anyone who does what is good is from God. Anyone who does what is evil has not seen God. (3 John 1:11)

Living a Christlike life is much easier said than done. Time after time, you find yourself faltering due to your own fallibility, your natural tendency to sin and following your own head. Still, all this should not keep us from trying to bear God's image here on earth. Let's look at how Jesus was able to continuously demonstrate the greatness of our Father to the world:

- He was on God's side (John 3:21).
- He always acted according to His Father's will (John 4:34).
- He relied completely on His Father all through His life (John 5:19).

May you have the courage today to keep living in the Spirit, to do His will and to rely completely on your Father. If you do this, you will look like a copy of Jesus.

Lord Jesus, how would You have lived this day? Please show me. Amen.

Stand Up for What Is Right

He [Jesus] overturned the tables of the money changers and the benches of those selling doves, and would not allow anyone to carry merchandise through the temple courts. (Mark 11:15-16)

Jesus certainly was not Someone you could call a pushover. From as early as the age of twelve, He stood up for what He believed in. He never hesitated to disagree with others, to take a stand and voice His opinion or to reveal the mysteries of His Father to the people.

Probably one of the most surprising things that Jesus did was to cleanse the temple of unholy practices. He was so upset that the people dared to misuse His Father's place of worship that He chased them out.

Are you willing to stand up for what is right, like Jesus did? Do you take a stand against the things that dishonor Him? Are you willing to say no or to disagree with others for the sake of His holy name?

Let's pray that we will have the courage to show
the world that we live only for Him – at the right
time, in the right place and in the right way.

Forgive me, Lord, for not always honoring You. Help me to fight for You. Amen.

Learn from Him

Instruct the wise and they will be wiser still; teach the righteous and they will add to their learning. (Proverbs 9:9)

There is no shame in stumbling and falling. We all sometimes fall face first in the mud of sin. Before we can stop ourselves, we say the wrong thing, we hurt people, we fall for temptation or we do something that disgraces Christ's image. That is when we are faced with a decision: do you stay down in the mud or do you admit that you are "dirty" and learn from your mistake?

When David committed adultery, he was a muddy child of God … until he repented of his transgression and received forgiveness. When Peter denied Jesus, he immediately realized that he had turned his back on his Master. And yet, he was able to learn from his mistake and serve God in a wonderful way. Paul made a 180-degree turn on the road to Damascus and changed his life of rebellion against God around and started living all out for God.

May you have the courage today to stand
up and live as a cleansed child of God,
just like the heroes of faith from the Bible.

Father, please forgive me and teach me. Amen.

Cultivate a Christlike Character

We know that suffering produces perseverance; perseverance, character; and character, hope … (Romans 5:3-4)

Maintaining healthy relationships with other people is a sensitive matter! Just when we think that everything is going well, some or other misunderstanding, displeasure or conflict pops up. Before we know it, we are upset and unhappy because there is tension in the air.

It is in times like these that we can't help but wonder why we can't just live in perpetual peace with others. The answer lies in the fact that we are still camping out in fallible tents on this earth. Still, we should try to follow Jesus' way of doing things and try to make it our own every day:

- Decide to express peace and forgiveness towards others today.
- Try to accept everyone as they are and reach out to them.
- Live with the desire to serve others with a pure heart.

When you live out a Jesus-personality in this way, you will receive grace to introduce real peace into the most awkward situations. Pray that something of His heavenly love will be in you today.

Teach me Your wisdom and Your peace, O God. Amen.

Make Peace

For He Himself is our peace ... (Ephesians 2:14)

Do you also find that life is difficult when there is tension between you and someone else? Because when that is the case, we often feel like we can't even concentrate on anything else.

Conflict and relationship problems are like rats that gnaw on our hearts and devour every last little bit of peaceableness. The problem is that peace doesn't just happen. Establishing peace often requires quite a bit of hard work; like working on changing our attitude, our understanding, our forgiveness and our unconditional love for others. And when we are still angry or hurt, it is not easy to do this "work" at all.

It is in times like these that we need to surrender our hearts to the working of the Holy Spirit by asking the following: "Lord, please help me to understand. Teach me how to be more compassionate and replace my spirit of rebellion with Your peace. Place some of Your great love in my heart: Your love that is able to forgive and accept others unconditionally. Please help me, Lord, I can't do this on my own!"

Do not allow unease and strife to gnaw away
at your heart, do not allow pieces of your heart
to be lost in that way. Give your whole heart to
the Spirit of God and ask Him to make the peace.

It is not easy to do what You ask, Lord, so please help me. Amen.

Break Down the Walls

[Jesus] has made the two groups one and has destroyed the barrier, the dividing wall of hostility. (Ephesians 2:14).

When there is conflict between people, they tend to build nearly un-surpassably high walls in and around their hearts. These walls are like barriers that keep us from forgiving, reaching out and reconciling with each other. Once this has happened, it is very difficult to once again have a healthy relationship.

Christ knew that we humans are quick to build walls that separate us from other people. And that is exactly why He came to earth. Not only did He come to reconcile us to God, but also so that we can live in peace with one another.

Peace is a flower that starts growing in the hearts of people who have been touched by the Holy Spirit.

Before you try to make peace with others, ask
the Holy Spirit to come and break down the wall
of strife that you erected in your own heart.
Only then will you be able to truly reconcile.

Break down every last brick of hate, bitterness and unforgiveness in my heart, please Lord. Amen.

Build Others Up

The name of the righteous is used in blessings, but the name of the wicked will rot. (Proverbs 10:7)

It is never nice to be criticized. It always feels like some form of rejection. It usually makes us feel defiant and like we just want to go and sulk in our own little corner, away from everyone else.

Now, it is true that criticism can sometimes be valid, fair and constructive, but at other times, it may be unfair and destructive. When someone criticizes you, always ask yourself the following question: Is the criticism fair and what can I learn from it? Do that and then make peace with it.

On the other hand, when you need to admonish someone, pray and ask the Spirit to help you do it fairly and with love so that you can make a constructive and positive contribution to someone else's life.

Let's pray and ask the Spirit to show us in all instances
what He cares about most and that He would help us
to act accordingly. Then we will do what Thomas Fuller
advises: "Govern thy life and thy thoughts as if the whole
world were to see the one, and read the other."

Father, help me to plant Your words in the hearts of others. Amen.

Bear the Fruit of the Spirit

"If you love Me, keep My commands." (John 14:15)

When I read through the list of the fruits of the Spirit in Galatians 5:22-23, I just know that I lack spiritual fruit. Things like love, joy, peace, forbearance, kindness, goodness, faithfulness, gentleness and self-control are not all part of who I am. It takes a life permanently lived in and through the Spirit to be able to continuously display these characteristics. And that is no easy feat! But it is exactly what Christ asks of us. To live out the true image of Christ on earth, we must display those characteristics.

Today, be encouraged by the words of James as he writes: "Let perseverance finish its work so that you may be mature and complete, not lacking anything" (James 1:4). The Spirit knows our weaknesses and He wants to help us to do the right thing in every situation. For that reason, we can repeatedly ask Him to help us to do our Father's will.

Pray without ceasing that you will be filled with the Holy Spirit so that you can be spiritually rich.

Jesus, please give me the courage to do what You ask. Amen.

Be His Letter

You show that you are a letter from Christ, the result of our ministry, written not with ink but with the Spirit of the living God.
(2 Corinthians 3:3)

When Jesus ascended to heaven, He left us, His children, with a great responsibility to bear. He basically gave us the authority to be His messengers here on earth. Messengers who are supposed to deliver life-letters of faith, hope and love to other people.

What does your life-letter look like? Can others read about Christ's great love for humanity in it? Do you think the way you live gives other people hope? Has someone accepted Christ because you told him or her about the love of Jesus?

The world reads our lives like a letter and it is supposed to tell them how much we love our Master. They follow the narrative, they watch us to see how we handle crises, they listen to our words, they feel our hearts and then … they decide whether or not they want to get to know the One who we have dedicated our lives to.

Let's pray that we will deliver life-letters
that say, "Jesus lives!" every day.

Lord, I am but a letter full of spelling errors. Will You please come and correct my life so that I can live out the pure language of Your love? Amen.

Persevere in Faith

*But we do not belong to those who shrink back and are destroyed,
but to those who have faith and are saved. (Hebrews 10:39)*

If you want to see Rome from the dome of St. Peter's Church, you are going to have to climb the stairs all the way to the top. If you climb only halfway up, the fact that you have progressed so far will not matter at all. Likewise, there are many things in this life that are good if you carry them through, but it means nothing if you stop before you have reached the top.

To follow in Christ's footsteps and to live out His example takes endless courage, self-discipline and perseverance. It requires constant effort: to get up again when you've fallen, to persevere despite difficult circumstances and to keep asking, "Lord Jesus, what would You do?"

According to William Barclay, the greatest honor that there is, is to have people say about you: she remained a loyal, sincere person to the end. May you reach your goal, the finish line, with your torch still burning!

Lord Jesus, help me to be just like You so that I can one day spend eternity with You. Amen.

May

The Courage to Stay on Your Feet

*"It is courage, courage and yet again courage
that raises the blood pressure of life to crimson.
Live your life courageously and put on a brave face in adversity."*

*Be strong and courageous. Do not be afraid or terrified
because of them, for the L*ᴏʀᴅ *your God goes with you;
He will never leave you nor forsake you.*

~ Deuteronomy 31:6

Do Not Become Discouraged

It is enough for students to be like their teachers, and servants like their masters. If the head of the house has been called Beelzebul, how much more the members of his household! (Matthew 10:25)

One moment everything seems to be going smoothly and the next … something happens and the entire picture changes.

It happens all too often that we try really hard to do the right thing … and then everything still goes wrong, despite our best efforts. At other times, it feels as if our problems and disappointments are snowballing and there seems to be no end to our misery. These are all very good reasons to become discouraged.

Fortunately, our Lord knows how easily we lose heart. Yes, Jesus knew exactly what He was talking about when He warned the disciples about the disappointments that are a part of life. And that is why He assured His followers of His eternal faithfulness time and again.

In Psalm 59:17 we see how the psalmist praises the Lord for the fact that we can always rely on Him. Know this today: the sun will shine again, because Your Father will make it happen.

Thank You, dear God, that I can always put my trust in You. Amen.

Know That He Is Good

Return to your rest, my soul, for the LORD has been good to you. For You, LORD, have delivered me from death, my eyes from tears, my feet from stumbling. (Psalm 116:7-8)

David grappled with many issues, just like you and I do. There were times when he was struck with terror, when he wanted to hide away because of his feelings of guilt and cried as if his heart was breaking.

He knew what it was like to be so crushed that you don't really feel like you can face another day. Because David went through all these very real human experiences and emotions, he was able to write such timeless psalms. David's psalms also convey the wonderful truth that we really can relax and know that God is in control, no matter what the circumstances are.

Remember our God is a God who forgives again and again, a God who is our safe fortress in times of trouble, who offers comfort in times of sadness and who will always pick us back up when we fall.

So, today, give your fragile heart to the God who has proven Himself to be faithful to His children all through the ages and know: He is also very good to you!

Thank You, Lord, for always being there for me. Amen.

Hold On to His Greatness

After I looked things over, I stood up and said to the nobles, the officials and the rest of the people, "Don't be afraid of them. Remember the Lord, who is great and awesome, and fight for your families, your sons and your daughters, your wives and your homes."
(Nehemiah 4:14)

After the Israelites' exile, they had to start over from scratch. Consequently, Ezra was tasked with rebuilding the temple that had been destroyed and Nehemiah had to repair the wall that was meant to offer the city protection.

Thanks to these two men's bravery and perseverance, the wall and the temple, as well as the hearts of the people, were restored. As a result, the people were once again able to safely come together to worship the Lord their God.

Ezra and Nehemiah had the courage to tackle seemingly impossible tasks and complete them successfully with the help of the Lord. And for that reason, the Lord Himself – the Lord who is forever always in control – led them to victory.

Maybe your own Jerusalem is also in ruins. Maybe you doubt that you will be able to rebuild the walls of your life. May you come to the realization today that your God can make the impossible happen.

Lord, I trust You with my whole life. Amen.

Be Proud Once Again

I said to them, "You see the trouble we are in: Jerusalem lies in ruins, and its gates have been burned with fire. Come, let us rebuild the wall of Jerusalem, and we will no longer be in disgrace."
(Nehemiah 2:17)

Some things in life just have a way of crushing our hearts. And then it takes a whole lot of courage not to stay down, but to get back up again. This is what the people must have felt like when they saw what Jerusalem looked like … until one man was brave enough to say: "Let's do this! Let's make sure that we can be proud of our city again."

Dear friend, with God at your side you are capable of anything. With Him and through Him, you can overcome any situation. Yes, He will repair whatever has been broken, rebuild whatever has been torn down, and heal human hearts that have been crushed.

Decide to be proud of who you are and what you do.
Take the bull by the horns and go and show the world
that, with God, you really can do the impossible.

Thank You, Master of my life, for healing and repairing whatever is broken. Amen.

Resist the Prophets of Doom

So we rebuilt the wall till all of it reached half its height, for the people worked with all their heart. (Nehemiah 4:6)

We all know those people … just when you have mustered enough courage to do something, they start telling you why you won't succeed. I'm sure that there must have also been prophets of doom in the time when Nehemiah and the people of Jerusalem were busy rebuilding the city wall.

The gloom-and-doomsters probably said things like: "Do they really think they'll be able to rebuild this wall?" Nehemiah, however, knew that it was God's will that the city wall be rebuilt and so he was sure that God would also help them do the impossible.

If God has shown you that you need to do something, then just do it. Do it while putting all your trust in Him and relying completely on Him. Do what you can and then leave the rest up to Him, He surely is more than capable. He is also faithful to those who obey Him. And therefore, His children will make a success of whatever tasks He assigns to them, despite opposition.

> Do not allow the world's prophets of doom
> to get you down. Do what you must do. And
> remember, the almighty God is your Father!

Thank You, dear Lord, for looking after Your faithful children.
Thank You for looking after me. Amen.

Keep Going

I answered them by saying, "The God of heaven will give us success. We His servants will start rebuilding ..." (Nehemiah 2:20)

Despite being very courageous and having faith, there comes a time during any big task or project when people get discouraged ... we start questioning ourselves and we wonder if maybe we weren't a little naïve or opportunistic when we decided to take it on.

While Jerusalem's walls were being rebuilt, there came a time when the workers felt weak and hopeless. They complained in Nehemiah 4:10: "The strength of the laborers is giving out, and there is so much rubble that we cannot rebuild the wall."

But once again, Nehemiah found the right words to encourage them as he said, "Remember the Lord, who is great and awesome" (Neh. 4:14). This helped them to once again take heart and keep going.

Brave friend, stay faithful to your calling while
you hold on tightly to the God that is greater
than any problem and mightier than any opposition
you may ever face. If you do this, you will triumph.

Here is my hand, Lord, lead me and carry me when I can't carry on. Demonstrate Your greatness through my life. Amen.

Show How Great He Is

So the wall was completed on the twenty-fifth of Elul, in fifty-two days. When all our enemies heard about this, all the surrounding nations were afraid and lost their self-confidence, because they realized that this work had been done with the help of our God. (Nehemiah 6:15-16)

Isn't it just wonderful to hear how God's people prevailed in the end? Those who are on God's side always win, even though it may seem impossible and in spite of setbacks and the world's negativity. Just like with Nehemiah and God's people in those days!

Nehemiah and his companions succeeded because he:

· had the courage to tackle a seemingly impossible task with God;
· was obedient and faithful to the Lord;
· kept relying on God despite fierce opposition; and
· had a devoted prayer life and frequently asked the Lord for advice and guidance.

Always hold on to hope. If you have lost hope, you
have lost everything. Remember that God is great!
And He manifests His greatness in and through faithful
believers. May your life demonstrate His greatness.

Lord, today I admit that I am nothing without You, but that I can do anything and everything with You. Amen.

Rebuild Your Heart

Brandish spear and javelin against those who pursue me. Say to me,
"I am your salvation." (Psalm 35:3)

There are numerous things that can make the walls of our hearts crumble to the ground. In difficult times, disappointment after disappointment seems to bulldoze them, people demolish each other with their words and actions and broken relationships leave us in ruins. When the walls of our hearts have been destroyed, we often tend to pity ourselves and try to hide behind what's left.

Yes, it doesn't matter how hard we try … as long as we are terrestrial beings, the walls of our hearts are bound to be flattened from time to time. The question, however, is: For how long are we going to sulk and what are we going to do to about it? Feeling sorry for yourself won't get you anywhere and neither will hiding amongst the ruins and to grumpily withdraw into a corner will only make things worse.

In times like these, ask the Holy Spirit to start rebuilding the walls of your heart brick by brick. Allow Him to draw your focus upward, to let you see the things in your life that are not broken and to help you find new hope.

Friend in Christ, get up and start rebuilding
your heart brick by brick today.

Thank You for strengthening me even now, Father. Amen.

MAY 9

Wait for Him to Open a Door

He settles the childless woman in her home as a happy mother of children. Praise the LORD! (Psalm 113:9)

We all know what it feels like to have a door slam shut in our face. We then typically experience a combination of different emotions: we feel dismayed, disappointed and utterly discouraged. How on earth could this happen? Why now? … you can't help but wonder as panic starts to set in.

Jesus' disciples felt like this at one stage too and then their Master said the following to them, "You will be hated by everyone because of Me, but the one who stands firm to the end will be saved. When you are persecuted in one place, flee to another" (Matt. 10:22-23).

Remember that God stays faithful to His children, no matter what the circumstances. Moreover, He will never shut one door without opening another door for you.

Trust your Father. He opens doors on
earth as well as heaven's gates for you.

Thank You, God of love, that You let me know today that You have something greater and better in store for me that I can look forward to. Amen.

Lift Up Your Head

Keep your mouth free of perversity; keep corrupt talk far from your lips. (Proverbs 4:24)

People have a way of hurting others. Whether it is knowingly or unknowingly, we all do and say things that catch others off guard, that leave them feeling dismayed and deeply hurt. Yes, we are all prone to dishing it out to others and unfortunately, sometimes, we are also on the receiving end.

When you realize that you were the one dishing it out, you have reason to bow your head in shame and ask for forgiveness. After all, you know how offended, bitter, angry and hurt you feel if you are the one on the receiving end.

Pray that you will be finely tuned into other people's feelings and needs today, that you would file the sharp edges of your heart so that you can respond with love and care. Also pray that when you find yourself on the receiving end, that you would handle the situation with wisdom, understanding and grace.

Lord, I sometimes struggle to get along well with others. Please help me with this. Amen.

Mend Broken Relationships

Vindicate me, LORD, for I have led a blameless life; I have trusted in the LORD and have not faltered. (Psalm 26:1)

You have the best intentions to get along with all people, to share God's love with others and to live in peace with those around you. Then why does it feel like you just can't manage to get it right? Why do misunderstandings occur, why do people hurt one another and why are there relationships that just get you down sometimes?

The reason is that we are sinful from birth, from the moment of conception, as the Word says in Psalms. Our natural tendency is to do the things that are against God's will and, sometimes, even against our own better judgment.

The best advice for relationships that have gone off track is to try and mend them as soon as possible. Getting yourself to forgive is the very first step. After that you will have to muster up the courage to confront the relevant person so that you can talk things out. And no, these kinds of conversations are never easy. Or nice. When we let the Holy Spirit direct the conversation, however, the outcome is usually surprisingly positive.

Broken relationships can be mended
with the help of the Holy Spirit.

Help me to forgive, reach out and make things right, Spirit of God. Amen.

Let Him Intercede

"Do not worry about what to say or how to say it. At that time you will be given what to say." (Matthew 10:19)

We have all been scared to death at one stage or another when we had to speak in public. At times we are afraid of the person we need to speak to, at other times we are afraid of the consequences that our conversation might bring about and sometimes we just don't know where to find the words to say. Never mind the panic that grips us when we have to speak in front of a crowd!

However, when you converse in the Spirit, you have the most wonderful Person on your side. And when the Holy Spirit is on your side, the Word promises you today: "But when they arrest you, do not worry about what to say or how to say it. At that time you will be given what to say, for it will not be you speaking, but the Spirit of your Father speaking through you" (Matt. 10:19-20).

Pray and ask the Holy Spirit to fill your heart and mind so that when you speak, He will speak through you. Then you don't have to fear the outcome!

Comforter, be my thoughts and my words today. Speak on my behalf. Amen.

See the New World

For our light and momentary troubles are achieving for us an eternal glory that far outweighs them all. (2 Corinthians 4:17)

It is only human to get caught up in the here and now – the temporary. This earthly here and now is the only frame of reference that we have and so our human minds find it hard to visualize heaven.

The aim of the letter that Paul wrote to the congregation in Corinth, was to teach them that suffering and setbacks are not the end of the world. He motivates his assertion with the fact that we, as believers that have been saved, live with an eternal hope while the Holy Spirit is there to strengthen us.

Sometimes when our circumstances leave us feeling like we just don't know what to do anymore, Jesus tells us the following with the passage from Scripture above: "Stop looking down; stop looking around; look up. Look at Me. Look at heaven!"

Thank You, Lord Jesus, for waiting at heaven's gates for me and thank You, Spirit of God, for taking my hand and leading me there. Amen.

Live with Hope

So we fix our eyes not on what is seen, but on what is unseen, since what is seen is temporary, but what is unseen is eternal.
(2 Corinthians 4:18)

The only way to get a different perspective on our present worldly circumstances, our problems and ourselves is to ask the Holy Spirit to give us heavenly eyes.

Eyes that do observe what is happening around us here on earth, but which are also hope-filled eyes because we know for sure that our Lord can make the impossible happen. Eyes that perceive that our great God is always in control, no matter what, and eyes that are fixed on the eternal because it's more important than the temporary.

When you are upset, the best solution is to make time to calm down in the presence of our Comforter. Then the Spirit will have the opportunity to assure you of His faithfulness.

Take a moment and be completely silent ... pray and ask the Father to paint you a picture of what it will look like when you sit on His lap as He tells you, "Do not worry so much, my dear child. I, the almighty God, am your God. And I will help you."

Thank You, dear Father, for being my God and that I can, therefore, be hopeful. Amen.

Be Honest

You turn things upside down, as if the potter were thought to be like the clay! Shall what is formed say to the one who formed it, "You did not make me"? Can the pot say to the Potter, "You know nothing"? (Isaiah 29:16)

We can hide nothing from God! To think that we can do whatever we want and He won't notice or He doesn't really care is naïve according to Isaiah.

The God who created us knows our every hidden thought, every unuttered word and every intended action. Moreover, He even knows what we are going to think, say and do in the future. So, it will not help to try and outrun God. He will always be one step ahead of us. It also displeases God if we are false, dishonest or hypocritical when we worship Him or when we repent.

God expects total honesty, openness and genuineness from us.

> Your Potter knows exactly how fragile you are.
> So therefore, turn to Him without reservations.

I know I sometimes try to run away from You, Father. Please forgive me for doing that. Help me to stay close to You, despite my fragility and sinfulness. Amen.

Pick up the Pieces

But we have this treasure in jars of clay to show that this all-surpassing power is from God and not from us. (2 Corinthians 4:7)

In his letter to the Corinthians, Paul writes that it doesn't matter how hard we try, we will always be fragile jars of clay. And because we are leading jars-of-clay-lives, we are fallible, imperfect and quite often guilty of sin.

And of course, we are embarrassed about our brokenness. It really is not nice to feel like a naughty child who got caught out when we disappoint God. Therefore, after having committed some or other sin, our natural tendency is to feel dejected and to agonize about it.

Despite everything, children of God always have hope. Our Lord Jesus Christ came to earth for that very reason – to make His jars-of-clay children whole again. And that is why we always have hope in this life, in spite of our brokenness. Norman Vincent Peale said, "Practice hope. As hopefulness becomes a habit, you can achieve a permanently happy spirit."

Dear jar of clay, don't remain in your brokenness.
Get up, look up and ask for forgiveness. Then you
will see Jesus' mercy-filled eyes looking back at you.
Courage means to get back up after every fall.

Thank You, Father, for always giving me the courage I need to start over. Amen.

Discover the Treasure inside You

But we have this treasure in jars of clay to show that this all-surpassing power is from God and not from us. We are hard pressed on every side, but not crushed; perplexed, but not in despair; persecuted, but not abandoned; struck down, but not destroyed.
(2 Corinthians 4:7-9)

Jesus knows that being jars of clay we are extremely fragile, that we easily fall and break in this life. For that reason, He did not leave us to fend for ourselves. He permanently placed His Spirit in our hearts. Did you hear that? Do you know what it means? It means that you have God – the greatest Treasure of all time – inside you!

Consequently, the Holy Spirit is inextricably part of your life. When you are being pushed around, broken, hopeless and doubtful; He stays in you. Even when you move away from Him at times or when you forget about Him or disappoint Him – He is still there. When you love God, you are known by Him and you are constantly on His mind.

May you come to the realization today that you are immeasurably valuable because He lives in you. So then go, lift up your head and live with abandon.

Thank You, Comforter, for spoiling me with so many heavenly riches by Your presence. Amen.

MAY 18

Wait on His Answers

We are hard pressed on every side, but not crushed; perplexed, but not in despair ... (2 Corinthians 4:8)

It doesn't matter how wise, clever or experienced we are, we are all faced with a question, problem or decision that we battle to solve. You ask God for guidance, seek the counsel of others and think about it until your head hurts … but you still can't get to the solution! Yes, even Paul admitted that he doesn't always know what to do.

When answers elude us, it is usually for a very good reason: We are not yet ready for the solution, or a few other things first need to fall in place, or our circumstances (or we!) need to change. Sometimes it's just not a good time for us to make a big decision. So in times like these, do not stop praying, asking and seeking God's will.

> One thing is certain, when we desire to do God's will, He will answer us. Maybe not when and how we think He should. But as He thinks best.

Thank You, all-wise God, that I know You know all things. Please help me to wait for Your answer. Amen.

Get Back Up Again

For in the day of trouble He will keep me safe in His dwelling; He will hide me in the shelter of His sacred tent and set me high upon a rock. (Psalm 27:5)

Disasters, nasty surprises, accidents and bad news often rain down on our hearts like the blows of a hammer. It crushes us and leaves us speechless and dismayed.

Part of the shock is, of course, the fact that it is so unexpected. The one moment everything is normal … and the next, nothing will ever be the same again. Your life is in chaos and everything around you seems to fall to pieces. *How am I going to survive this?* you think. *Will I ever want to get back up?* you wonder.

Dear friend, when life has knocked you down, there is no easy way to get back up again. But remember that God is in control and He will lift you up.

God is the God of disaster-stricken children; people who are just too broken to get back up. In times like these, you have to know: your God is still in control. He can and will carry you through and He does want to see you get back up and live a joyful life.

Thank You, Lord, for being the lifter of my head. Amen.

When You Can't Carry On!

"The poor and needy search for water, but there is none; their tongues are parched with thirst. But I the Lord will answer them; I, the God of Israel, will not forsake them." (Isaiah 41:17)

Do you know when God steps in? When you and I have absolutely nothing left! Yes, when we are so empty, broken and despondent that we are left speechless in our search for answers, that is when God's power is at its greatest.

How do you feel today? Are you down and does it feel like you just want to throw in the towel? Do you feel like you are at your wit's end, discouraged, powerless … hopeless? Then know, when you are weak, then you are strong. Even though you feel at a loss right now, you do have wisdom. And He is busy substituting your discouragement with His hope.

When you run out of words, He intercedes for you; when your tears fall, He wipes them away. When you say, "I can't," He tells you, "I can!"

Live your life step by step … moment by moment;
knowing that He can do everything for you, and He will.

Spirit of God, I thank You that I can because You can. Amen.

Fight Back

Jacob was in love with Rachel and said, "I'll work for you [Laban] seven years in return for your younger daughter Rachel."
(Genesis 29:18)

Sometimes life just leaves us stunned … just think about this example of Jacob who had worked for Laban for seven years to marry Rachel, the woman he was in love with. He was loyal and kept his side of the bargain and must have been overjoyed when he was finally able to marry her.

However, he was in for the surprise of his life when he woke up the morning after their wedding night and found that the woman under the veil was in fact Leah, Rachel's sister … and that he had worked for seven years to marry her instead of Rachel!

Jacob was faced with a choice. Was he going to give up or try again? He decided to enter into another agreement with Laban and so he worked an additional seven years to be able to marry Rachel, the woman of his dreams.

What will you do when life catches you off guard?
Will you choose to remain hopeful and try again?

Lord Jesus, make me strong enough to always try again. I know that You are always with me! Amen.

Keep Standing Strong

That same day [Laban] removed all the male goats that were streaked or spotted, and all the speckled or spotted female goats (all that had white on them) and all the dark-colored lambs, and he placed them in the care of his sons. (Genesis 30:35)

People have not really changed much through the years. And so there will always be those people who love us and that we can trust as well as those who deceive us, betray us, let us down … and even steal from us. They may steal earthly possessions or even our heart's peace.

In Genesis 30:25-43, we see that Laban tried to take Jacob in for a second time by stealing from him in a very cunning way. Jacob, however, stays on the straight and narrow and does what is right. How ironic that Laban actually shoots himself in the foot with his underhand actions and Jacob is ultimately the one who gets the strong animals and who becomes richer and richer.

> When people's deceitfulness catches you off
> guard, you must not lose heart. Stay on the right
> track. When you do that, God will be on your side.
> And what more could you possibly want?

Faithful God, please help me to stay pure and honorable and to stay on the straight-and-narrow road of life. Amen.

Be Reconciled

Then he [Joseph] threw his arms around his brother Benjamin and wept, and Benjamin embraced him, weeping. And he kissed all his brothers and wept over them. (Genesis 45:14-15)

Anger, bitterness and unforgiveness have a way of pulling us down. The angrier we get, the more we plot revenge … and the less we are able to love. In this way, we dig a grave of bitterness for ourselves in which we remain unhappy and depressed.

It is never easy to forgive. But it is always worth it. Because when we forgive, the dam walls of our hatred-filled hearts break and the poison of bitterness runs out. When these cropped-up emotions flow out of us it brings relief, and peace can once again be established in our lives.

Henri Nouwen said, "Forgiveness is the cement of community life. Forgiveness holds us together through good and bad times, and it allows us to grow in mutual love."

Who do you need to make peace with in your life?
Who needs to hear you say, "I forgive you"? Who does
God want you to reconcile with? Will you do it today?

Help me to forgive completely, Lord, and teach me the way of reconciliation. Amen.

Don't Play God

But Joseph said to them, "Don't be afraid. Am I in the place of God? You intended to harm me, but God intended it for good to accomplish what is now being done, the saving of many lives. So then, don't be afraid. I will provide for you and your children." And he reassured them and spoke kindly to them. (Genesis 50:19-21)

Jacob had passed away. And Joseph's brothers were living in fear. Surely Joseph was going to make use of his chance to take revenge on them for selling him as a slave. However, Joseph had chosen to do things differently long before. He had already forgiven them years ago. So therefore, he is able to reassure them, without hesitation, that he has nothing but love in his heart for them.

Do you think that there is someone in your life who is waiting for you to take revenge on them? Someone whom you can surprise by forgiving them? Or is there still a part of your heart that secretly wishes that person will one day get what they deserve?

Decide today to forgive completely and leave the rest in God's hands. After all, Jesus forgave you unconditionally.

Lord, please help me to remember that You are the One who will avenge and that I must forgive. Yes, Lord, You are God and I am not. Amen.

The Courage to Try Again

The LORD says, "I will guide you along the best pathway for your life. I will advise you and wath over you." (Psalm 32:8)

Most people have the genuine intention of being "a good person". Deep down in our hearts, we all really do want to do the right thing, treat others with respect and live in peace with one another.

So, when our actions go against the grain of our intentions – either because we are under a lot of pressure, or because we are irritated or due to disappointment – we feel like a failure. Then you can't help but wonder, "Why can't I get it right? Why can't I make a success of my life?"

Dear friend, making a mistake does not make you a failure. Giving up, however, does. That is why God put only 24 hours in every day. He gives us the opportunity to try again every morning when the sun rises and fills the earth with rays of hope. It doesn't matter what your yesterdays were like, when the day breaks, you once again have the chance to walk the straight and narrow. Because God's mercies are new every morning.

God will never, ever give up on you. So therefore, you can always – despite everything – try again!

Thank You, perfect Creator, for continually recreating me. Recreate me once more today. Amen.

Leave the Past in the Past

He will bring me out into the light; I will see His righteousness.
(Micah 7:9)

We have a human tendency to keep looking back. How often do we cling to the past? We dwell on what we should have done, what we should not have done, what could have been, what we had wanted … and then?

If events or people have ever knocked you down, you will know how hard it is to take off your old shoes and to continue on your journey of life with new ones. After all, yesterday's shoes are worn in and comfortable, while the new ones still pinch you.

Leave the past behind. It is over. Pray and ask the Holy Spirit
to help you live for today. Because today is all you have.

Father God, help me to let go of all my yesterdays so that I can truly be alive in my tomorrows. Amen.

Do Something

Do not merely listen to the word, and so deceive yourselves. Do what it says. (James 1:22)

A comfort zone is exactly what the name says. It is a familiar place where you feel safe … where you are comfortable. And all too often it is also a place where we tend to stay for too long. The fact of the matter is that it is hard for God to work with comfort zone Christians. They are usually not willing to sacrifice their own comfort for Him or for other people. They are too set in their ways of doing nothing.

Where do you think you are? Are you sitting on a comfortable chair of idleness? Or are you willing to go the extra mile, to sacrifice a little, to give away some of your time or even a valued possession? It is never easy to get out of your comfort zone and to move to a place that asks something of you, that requires sacrifice. However, the Word tells us that that is exactly what the Father expects of us.

Decide to get out of your comfort zone
and to do what He asks of you today.

Lord, help me to remember that an uncomfortable task is often so much more rewarding. Amen.

Get Back Up Every Time

Who is a God like You, who pardons sin and forgives the transgression
of the remnant of His inheritance? You do not stay angry forever but
delight to show mercy. (Micah 7:18)

You know that God loves you and that you have been saved by His grace. You know that there was a time when you were absolutely sure that He redeemed you and that you are His beloved child. And then, one day, you started to wonder: *Have I not disappointed Him one too many times? Is my sin not too much and too great? Is it really true that He will forgive me and accept me unconditionally time after time?*

When you start to think and feel like this, Satan is very happy with the way things are going, because that is exactly where he wants you: down on the ground, wallowing in your feelings of guilt and doubt. And he also likes to kick you when you're down, making you doubt even more.

> Child of God, do not allow Satan to make you doubt the fact
> that you have been saved. God does love you and therefore
> you are saved and so you can get back up again every time.

Thank You, forgiving God, for not staying angry with me. Amen.

Throw Your Sin in the Sea

You will again have compassion on us; you will tread our sins underfoot and hurl all our iniquities into the depths of the sea (Micah 7:19)

If you have given your life to God, if you admit that Jesus Christ is Lord and if you believe that He will save you, then God has hurled all your sin into the depths of the sea and there is a sign that reads: No fishing. That means that neither you nor He will ever have to think about it again.

How sad that even though the children of God have heard this a thousand times, they still often go out to sea to go and fish for their sin! Are you one of them? Do you often think back on the things that you did wrong, the things that you are ashamed of and do you then wonder if God really forgave all of it?

When God has forgiven you, He does not look back.
According to Him, it is over and done with!
So why would you want to bring it back up?

Thank You, Lord, for forgiving and forgetting! Please help me to also forgive myself. Amen.

He Wants to Bless You

"The Lord bless you and keep you; the Lord make His face shine on you and be gracious to you; the Lord turn His face toward you and give you peace." (Numbers 6:24-26)

You serve a great God! A God who is majestic in His omnipotence, His love and His grace. Yes, there is literally no limit to His sovereignty and goodness. And this very God keeps an eye on you, His beloved child, every day – eyes filled with the greatest compassion and love.

Today, drink deeply of this wonderful promise of grace. Let it sink deep into your heart so that you:

- can remember that He is your security in times of doubt;
- will know that He will help you to get back up in times of failure;
- will keep holding onto His hand in times of trouble;
- will know that He comforts you in times of tribulation.

> Your God wants only the very best for you.
> So, He will answer your prayers in His time
> and in His way. He will also give you peace,
> the peace that surpasses all understanding.

Thank You, Father God, for taking care of me and for blessing me abundantly. Amen.

Accept His Care

I will make rivers flow on barren heights, and springs within the valleys. (Isaiah 41:18)

We all go through stages in our lives that for some or other reason seem dry and barren … in such times, you must know this: it does not matter where you find yourself on your journey of life, how many things seem uncertain or what disasters come your way; your God is in control and He will look after you.

He may not do what you had hoped He would and He might take a lot longer to give you the breakthrough that you so desperately need. But still, you need to put all your trust in your faithful God. Follow Him blindly. Without seeing the answer and without knowing what tomorrow might bring, just keep following Him and keep moving forward courageously.

Remember this promise: "And will not God bring about justice for His chosen ones, who cry out to Him day and night? Will He keep putting them off?" (Luke 18:7)

Thank You for also being with me on the barren plains of my life, Lord. Amen.

June

The Courage to Cry

*"Remember that the tears of life belong to the interlude,
not the finale, of your story."*

~ Alice Huff

*He will not let your foot slip – He who watches over you
will not slumber; indeed, He who watches over Israel
will neither slumber nor sleep. The LORD watches over you.*

~ Psalm 121:3-5

The Art of Crying

May our Lord Jesus Christ Himself and God our Father, who loved us and by His grace gave us eternal encouragement and good hope, encourage your hearts and strengthen you. (2 Thessalonians 2:16-17)

Some women (like me!) are experts at being vulnerable. We are easily brought to tears and our hearts can literally cry about anything. Our emotions are really fragile and so we can say that we have successfully mastered the art of crying. Crying with abandon and inconsolably!

Then there are also women who appear to be less affected by the storms of life and seem to be able to handle every situation gracefully and with self-control … even when their hearts are breaking.

It doesn't matter how strong your heart is, the fact of the matter is that you may cry. God created us with the ability to cry. And He has a very good reason for it. Quite often, He can only break through our walls of pretense when we are sad and broken before Him.

It is in times of brokenness that your Father gets the chance to hold you in His arms like a young child while He whispers softly in your ear, "You are precious to Me." Do you hear Him?

Thank You, Father, for holding me tighter than ever when I cry. Amen.

Shed Tears of Joy

Joseph had his chariot made ready and went to Goshen to meet his father Israel. As soon as Joseph appeared before him, he threw his arms around his father and wept for a long time. (Genesis 46:29)

We sometimes cry because we feel intense pain or longing in our hearts. At other times, we cry because we feel sorry for ourselves or for someone else. We may even cry due to frustration or anger. And then there are also tears of joy.

These are tears that spontaneously run down our cheeks when we feel proud of a loved one, when we hear good news, when someone spoils us unexpectedly and … when we come home to someone we have missed dearly.

Just like Jacob and Joseph, father and son, who thought that they would never see each other again, but were ultimately reunited and could throw their arms around one another again. How overwhelmingly tender that moment must have been …

> May we possess the ability to bless others with tears of joy, because we enrich their lives with something special through our love and compassion.

Comforter, please show me how to let streams of joy flow to other people. Amen.

Live through the Pain

In You, LORD my God, I put my trust. (Psalm 25:1)

Losing a loved one will always be one of the most heart-breaking ex-periences. The emotions of mourning and grief run deeper than words can express. We all go through intense – and very important – stages of grief. Initially, there is denial when we try to bargain with God, then the anger and depression set in. We all typically pass through these stages before we finally come to accept the loss.

When the worst happens and you lose a loved one, you will most probably have to work through your intense emotions on your own, even if you have a support system. There will be times when the pain will feel unbearable, when the loss will feel indescribably great and when you will miss the person so much that it feels as if your heart is never going to mend.

In times of intense sadness and pain, remember this, there is One who knows and understands and He is always by your side. It is your heavenly Father who once had to look on as His beloved Son died on the cross.

Walk the road of pain step by step with Him. He understands!

Heavenly Father, please wrap me in Your loving arms today. Amen.

Mourning the Loss of a Loved One

The king [David] was shaken. He went up to the room over the gateway and wept. (2 Samuel 18:33)

A parent's love for his or her child is unconditional, self-sacrificing and forgiving. Just like David's love for his son. Even when his very own son revolted and rose up in arms against his father, David told his men not to harm him.

That is why he was so crushed when he got the news that his son had died. We read that he walked up and down saying, "O my son Absalom! My son, my son Absalom! If only I had died instead of you – O Absalom, my son, my son!" (2 Sam. 18:33).

Oh, it is so terrible … so excruciatingly painful when a loved one dies. That is why we are, initially, inconsolable and overcome by grief. Broken! Raw! Miserable! Shattered!

Dear friend, know that your Father is closer to you than ever before when you are crushed and broken; that He cries with you for your loss and that He is holding you tightly – oh, so tightly.

Spirit of God, I just don't have the words to say how I feel … please pray for me. Amen.

Allow Him to Comfort You

Then they cried out to the Lord in their trouble, and He delivered them from their distress. He led them by a straight way to a city where they could settle. (Psalm 107:6-7)

All of us reach a point in our lives when we wonder where on earth we are going to get the courage to face another day. We grapple with all kinds of questions; for example, is God still with me? Will He really make all things work for good? Then why do I feel so discouraged? Is there any meaning to life?

Many, many people have felt this way. Think of Job whose body and spirit were broken as a result of all the losses he had suffered, or Jesus who cried bitterly when His friend Lazarus died, or Mary whose heart broke when she looked on as her Son was hanging on the cross. And yet, all these broken people found the strength to carry on … because God dried their tears.

God always comforts His broken children with great compassion. So you can carry on, knowing that He will bless you with His loving goodness and eternal care every day of your life, no matter what happens to you.

Take life one day at a time, knowing that
He will comfort you without end.

Thank You, Lord, that I can just pour out all my emotions to You. You understand. Amen.

Love While You Still Can

Let us love one another, for love comes from God. (1 John 4:7)

Maurice Maeterlinck writes, "When we lose one we love, our bitterest tears are called forth by the memory of hours when we loved not enough."

How many times have you heard of someone who had just lost a loved one, and blaming themselves for the things they said and did or didn't say and do while that person was still alive? Thank God that we can be sure of this, because we are His children, we will one day have the opportunity to wholeheartedly love those who have departed from us. What a comforting thought! We will one day be together again.

However, never take one of your loved ones for granted. Keep on showering them with understanding, compassion and loving care. Let's live every day as if it is our loved ones' – or our – last day on earth. Ask the Holy Spirit to show you who needs your love today and then go and love them!

Love with abandon today … because you still can!

God of peace, let Your love flow through me today. Amen.

Remember That He Remembers!

How long, LORD? Will You forget me forever? How long will You hide Your face from me? (Psalm 13:1)

Pain makes people feel utterly alone. While your life is in pieces, the world appears to just carry on. The birds still sing in the trees, the sun still rises like every other morning … and everyone goes about their business as if nothing happened. Can't anyone see what you're going through? Is there not one person who understands how hard this is for you? Has everyone conveniently forgotten all about you while they carry on with their lives? One can't help but wonder.

Dear friend, there is one thing that you can be sure of. Your loving Father has not forgotten about you. When you cry, He will comfort your heart; when you call out to Him without words, the Spirit will intercede on your behalf and in times of desolation, He will fold His arms around you and wrap you in His presence. All you need to do is to focus your attention on Him and know: He is with you.

> When you are too weak to hold onto
> His hand, He will take hold of yours.

Thank You for not forgetting about me, Comforter God. Amen.

Comfort in Pain

"As a mother comforts her child, so will I comfort you; and you will be comforted over Jerusalem." (Isaiah 66:13)

Like lonely shadows on the wall … that is what missing someone feels like. You can see or sense that person, but you can't touch him or her. You can smell, hear and dream about him or her, but when you wake up, you are still alone.

You reminisce about the great times you had together, the laughter and the joys, the companionship, the love … Sometimes you wish that this could all just be a nightmare and that you could wake up and find that everything is back to the way it was; that the person you love so very much is still here.

You are lost in your longing!

God's grace offers us comfort in our pain and grief until it becomes less intense over time. And then our sadness gives way to longing. And there is no cure for missing someone. All you can do in these times of intense longing, is to hold on to and cherish the beautiful memories and be grateful for the time that you did get to spend together.

Share your longing with your Father. He really does understand and He will make even that more bearable.

Lord, I miss him/her! Please come and comfort this longing deep inside my heart. Amen.

JUNE 9

Keep on Living

Because of the LORD's great love we are not consumed, for His compassions never fail. They are new every morning; great is Your faithfulness. I say to myself, "The LORD is my portion; therefore I will wait for Him." (Lamentations 3:22-24)

The Nobel prize winner, Alexander Solzhenitsyn, spent many years as a prisoner in an inhumane Siberian labor camp. One day, he lost all hope and went to sit on a bench wishing that a soldier would just kill him right there and then. But then something happened: a fellow prisoner came and stood before him and drew the cross of Christ in the snow. It was a watershed moment in his life. He realized that God's love is warmer than the coldest snow and greater than any persecutor. And therefore, there is always hope – even in the worst of times.

God's compassions are new every morning!

He draws His love for you in the snow of your heart every single day and with that He tells you that you can trust Him again today!

In His Word, He promises to be there for you today, just like He was there for you yesterday and the day before that ... He promises to give you life in abundance.

Thank You for giving me the courage to live, Lord! Amen.

Know That He Is Coming!

"I have told you these things, so that in me you may have peace. In this world you will have trouble. But take heart! I have overcome the world." (John 16:33)

If God really can do anything, why does He allow pain and injustice in this world? Many of us have grappled with this question. The fact of the matter is that God gave us the privilege of free will and that is why things happen that are against God's will. Until Christ returns, we are engaged in a battle against evil and death. What we can be sure of, though, is that God will ultimately reach His goal, however long it takes.

Through His blood, Jesus triumphed over our archenemy, death. So, we can live our lives – in spite of all the pain in this world – assured of the fact that He will indeed one day return victoriously on the clouds. And then we will be free from all the injustice, pain, sadness and the sway of sin for all eternity.

Take courage, dear heart! Jesus is coming! We will
one day live without pain, fear or sin. In the meantime,
we have the Comforter who holds our hearts.

Thank You for coming again, Christ Jesus! Amen.

JUNE 11

Comfort Others

[The God of all comfort] comforts us in all our troubles, so that we can comfort those in any trouble with the comfort we ourselves receive from God. (2 Corinthians 1:4)

Pain, crises and worry have a way of making people withdraw from others. It is as if all your thoughts start to revolve only around your own pain and despair. James Jowett notes something important when he writes that, "God does not comfort us to make us comfortable, but to make us comforters." Paul confirms this when he says that God showers us with His goodness in our time of need … so that we can also do the same for others.

I know from experience that the moment I shift my focus away from myself to the needs of others, my own storm suddenly starts to look like smooth sailing, my own sadness is replaced with solace and my battle seems a lot less daunting.

> Let's resolve to be on the lookout for other people's distress – even in the midst of our own imperfect circumstances – let's reach out and say, "You can share your pain with me. It is safe to do so."

Teach me to be a comforter as well, Father. Amen.

Turn the Other Cheek

Let him sit alone in silence, for the LORD has laid it on him. Let him bury his face in the dust – there may yet be hope. Let him offer his cheek to one who would strike him, and let him be filled with disgrace. (Lamentations 3:28-30)

To keep quiet when people are treating you unfairly and unreasonably is certainly not easy. Our first reaction is to fight back, to defend ourselves and to give them a taste of their own medicine.

Well, every situation must be evaluated on its own merit. So, there will be times when the Father will want us to take a stand, to say what needs to be said and to stand up for Him, ourselves and others. But, there will also be times when we need to keep quiet and turn the other cheek.

Long ago, Jesus allowed other people to treat and judge Him unfairly and He endured torture and crucifixion without saying a word in protest … because that was His Father's will.

Pray and ask the Holy Spirit to direct you every day of your life. Ask Him to speak to you so that you can hear His voice and know when it is His will for you to speak and when you need to keep quiet.

Lord, show me Your way, please. Amen.

JUNE 13

Let Him Fight for You

You came near when I called You, and You said, "Do not fear." You, LORD, took up my case; You redeemed my life.
(Lamentations 3:57-58)

We are fallible people living in an imperfect world. That is why there is so much injustice, grief, pain and sadness.

One of the most painful experiences is when people – especially your friends – hurt you. Or when you have been done an injustice … and you are powerless to defend yourself. That is when you want to cry out like the author of Lamentations: "Do not close Your ears to my cry for relief" (3:56).

The wonderful thing is that God remains on your side – no matter what – if you do His will. He is your Legal Representative. He is the One who will take up your case, fight your cause and ensure that the verdict is in your favor. Even if your vindication only comes in the hereafter.

God has already entered into a contract with you,
His child, and it confirms: the Lord fights for me!

Thank You, Judge of my life, for reigning victorious. Amen.

He Will Stand by You

He will wipe every tear from their eyes. There will be no more death or mourning or crying or pain, for the old order of things has passed away. (Revelation 21:4)

The fact that innocent children get raped, people die unexpectedly, sickness tears down our bodies and that grief is our portion, is not God's will. No, God is not One who doles out suffering in His sovereignty. God is the One who stands by His children in their times of distress, just like He promised.

When people go against God's will and hurt others in the process, God stands by those in crisis. When sickness, pain and even death come our way, God is there to carry us through it all – continually and unconditionally!

God makes a difference to the distress of those who put their trust in Him. When you hold onto His hand in all circumstances, you will experience how He wraps you in peace and gives you closure while He softly comforts you and stands by you with compassion.

Trust the God who will one day make everything new and painless.

Thank You for wrapping Your arms around me and cherishing me. Amen.

Cry It Out

Then the LORD God made a woman from the rib He had taken out of the man. (Genesis 2:22)

We all know the story of the angel who asked the Creator why He spent so much time creating the woman. After God explained to the angel how very intricate and special He had to make the woman so that she could fulfill all her roles, the angel was surprised to see a tear on her cheek. "But there is a mistake," the angel said, "why is your creation leaking?"

"A woman must be able to handle so much and carry so many emotions inside her that she needs an outlet, a way to express her womanhood," God answered. "Tears are for when a woman's soul overflows. It is a sign that she is still soft, vulnerable and … truly woman, even though she is also competent and strong. When a woman cries, it is her deep inner being that spontaneously spills over."

God knew that with your strong character, exceptional capabilities and unfathomable ability to persevere, He also needed to equip you with floodgates; floodgates in the walls of your soul so that you can sometimes … just spill over.

Thank You, Creator, that I can sometimes just cry it out. Amen.

Hear His Voice

You led your people like a flock by the hand of Moses and Aaron.
(Psalm 77:20)

We often wonder why God allows bad things to happen to good people. The answer to this question is not easy or simple.

God is God and, therefore, we will never understand His ways. All we can do is to hold onto the fact that God knows what He is doing and that there is a reason for everything. We do not go through suffering in vain.

There may be many reasons why distress crosses our path; it may be God's way of getting us back on the right track. Or maybe our Lord wants to use the time of tears to help us grow, to strengthen our faith or to draw us closer to Him. It may also be that He wants to use our pain to touch and change other people's lives. How would we know?

When you are hurting, it is the perfect time to go and sit down at His feet and listen for His voice. Do it. In His time, He will give you the answers to all your questions.

Lord, I don't always understand, but I know You are in control. Amen.

JUNE 17

When You Don't Understand

Jesus replied, "You do not realize now what I am doing, but later you will understand." (John 13:7)

Peter had a close relationship with his Master for three years. One can assume that he knew Jesus pretty well. And yet, when Jesus wrapped a towel around His waist and started to wash His disciples' feet, Peter was dumbfounded. He just couldn't understand what He was doing!

Being a believer and knowing God does not mean that we will necessarily always understand Him or what He is busy doing in our lives. No, our Lord's way of doing things will not always make sense to us. He also does not explain everything to us just because we know Him … and He doesn't have to, because He is God!

We all go through times in our lives when our Father's ways seem strange and incomprehensible. And then we simply need to keep trusting Him. He knows what He is doing, because He really is the all-wise God.

Trust Him, even if you don't understand a thing!

Master, help me to trust You blindly with my life. Amen.

Deal with Disappointment

And hope does not put us to shame, because God's love has been poured out into our hearts through the Holy Spirit, who has been given to us. (Romans 5:5)

Have you cried your heart out because you were bitterly disappointed? Maybe you hoped and believed you would get a specific thing, that things would work out well and that you would be successful … just to be knocked down by disappointment. Or maybe you trusted someone wholeheartedly and he or she let you down.

J. Wallace Hamilton writes the following with regard to disappointment: "The increase of suicides, alcoholics, and even some forms of nervous breakdowns is evidence that many people are training for success when they should be training for failure. Failure is far more common than success; poverty is more prevalent than wealth; and disappointment more normal than arrival."

> Knowing and serving God does not safeguard us from disappointment. What He, however, does do is to give us the strength to get back up after every fall, to try again after every failed attempt, and to keep striving for victory after every unexpected defeat.

Thank You, God, for picking me up when I feel like staying down. Amen.

Live with Joy

For this God is our God for ever and ever; He will be our Guide even to the end. (Psalm 48:14)

When things keep going wrong and we are faced with disappointment from all sides, it is easy to start losing faith in ourselves and others and start questioning the fairness of life.

Thank God that, in spite of all the crookedness of this world, we serve one amazingly faithful Father. We have Someone who assures us again and again – through His Word, His Spirit and His life – that He will never, ever, ever let us down. That is more than enough reason to rejoice and celebrate.

Paul writes to the church in Rome, "Not only is this so, but we also boast in God through our Lord Jesus Christ, through whom we have now received reconciliation" (Rom. 5:11).

Let's thank and praise our faithful God – the Light
that dispels all darkness; the unshakable Rock of Ages,
yes, the Righteous One who bought us at a price.

You are the One in whom I place all my hope, great God. Amen.

Walk the Straight and Narrow

"The Holy Spirit will teach you at that time what needs to be said."
(Luke 12:12)

Sometimes other people can get us down. They shock, disappoint and even scare us or make us cry. Because we are human, we hurt one another, we misunderstand, we behave poorly and we don't always do the right thing.

Because we are daily at the mercy of our sinful nature, so to speak, it is of the utmost importance that we strive to be Spirit-filled every moment of every day. When we are tuned into our God's voice, we will:

- in all circumstances, know what the truth is deep down inside;
- receive His wisdom in difficult situations;
- have the insight to treat others with understanding;
- have compassion and empathy for other people, and
- walk the straight and narrow always and in all instances.

Obey your Father every moment of your day. Then you can tackle any situation or approach any person with confidence, knowing that He will guide you.

God, show me the right way to go, please. Amen.

"I've Had Enough!"

"I will not," he answered, but later he changed his mind and went.
(Matthew 21:29)

Here in Matthew we find the story of a father who had two sons. When he asked the first to lend a hand with the farm work, the son replied without hesitation, "I will not."

We also have to admit that there are days when we just want to shout to the world, "I don't want to deal with all your nonsense anymore. I am tired of everyone and everything!"

In a time when life puts innumerable demands on a woman, when stress and our fast-paced lives are driving us into the ground, this typical feeling of "I've had enough" is quite understandable and to be expected.

When we feel like this, we need to seriously implore the Father to guide our hearts, thoughts and our lives for us so that we can stay in control of our emotions.

Pray today and ask Him to guide your heart – more than ever.

Spirit of God, please help me to control my emotions when I feel I've had enough. Amen.

See the Stars

My comfort in my suffering is this: Your promise preserves my life.
(Psalm 119:50)

Have you ever been so down and out that human comfort or words could not help you? That is when we need to look past the here and now; when we must look out the windows of our soul into the night … and focus our eyes on the stars in heaven. That is when we need to know: God is there!

Helmut Thielicke wrote: "He who dares to live in this way, in the name of this miracle, in the name of this opened heaven will see the glory of God, the comforting stars of God shining in the darkest valleys of his life and will wait with all the joyful expectancy of a child for the next morning where the Father will be waiting with His surprises. For God is always positive. He makes all things new. And the lighted windows of the Father's house shine brightest in the far country where all our 'blessings' have been lost."

> Live today with childlike joy, because you know
> that the Lord's greatness is with you. He has
> promised to be your faithful Father, hasn't He?

Hallelujah, Lord God! I praise Your holy name! Amen.

Plagued by Frustration

This is how we know that we belong to the truth and how we set our hearts at rest in His presence. (1 John 3:19)

We usually cry out of frustration when things have gone too far. Our crying is typically preceded by a long chain of events where things just kept going wrong. It is when we just feel sick and tired of it all as well as discouraged because it seems like we're constantly fighting with our backs against the wall!

I think our dear Lord Jesus has a great deal of understanding for what we feel like when frustrations get the better of us. He must have often felt the same way when people came to Him with their silly arguments, when no one seemed to understand Him or when He was faced with difficult circumstances.

He most probably also complained in solitude to His Father about the "small" world He had to live in and He may even have cried about mankind's injustice and lack of understanding.

Even if no one else understands you, He will; if the world pushes your buttons, you can find rest with Him and if you feel like you just can't do this anymore, He will do it for you. Because your God really does understand!

Thank You for understanding me without me having to explain myself, Lord. And thank You for helping me. Amen.

Just Be Yourself

If our hearts condemn us, we know that God is greater than our hearts, and He knows everything. (1 John 3:20)

The fact that God knows everything about us and even knows us better than we know ourselves can sometimes be a scary thought, but I mostly find the idea very reassuring.

At least there is one Person who knows me, accepts me and loves me … just as I am. Someone with whom my secrets – and my heart – are safe. I can complain to Him, share my joys with Him, be honest with Him about my doubts and … cry in front of Him.

The wonderful thing about our heavenly Father is that we don't need to explain everything to Him in detail because He already knows everything. We can leave our uncertainties with Him, because He knows them. We can confess our sins to Him, because He wants to forgive us. We can pour out our hearts to Him, because He wants to comfort us.

Remember, it doesn't matter what you're struggling with inside – with your Father, you can … just be yourself.

Thank You that I can be open and honest with You about how I feel. Amen.

Cry about Your Sin

Forgive my hidden faults. Keep Your servant also from willful sins.
(Psalm 19:12-13)

We all sometimes go against God's will. Even the great heroes of our faith, people like Moses, Abraham, Jonah, David and Peter all bitterly disappointed God. For as long as we are human, we will – unfortunately – let our heavenly Father down from time to time.

It is also a typical human reaction to try and hide from God when we have behaved in a way that is against His will. We are quick to turn our backs on Him because we feel ashamed and scared. The Word also tells us that we have very good reason to cry when we have committed sin. Because through sin, we cause damage to our lives and quite possibly also to the lives of those around us.

It is important to realize the following; when you go to God with genuine remorse and in true repentance, He will welcome you with open arms. Yes, God does accept I'm-sorry-tears and He will forgive you on the spot.

Do not hide from God if you feel ashamed of what you've done. Confess your sins and repent and then know: His forgiveness is all-encompassing.

Here I am, Lord, sinful, broken and ashamed. Please make me whole again. Amen.

JUNE 26

Turn to Him

This is what the Sovereign LORD, the Holy One of Israel, says: "In repentance and rest is your salvation, in quietness and trust is your strength." (Isaiah 30:15)

God is straightforward about what He expects of us. He wants us to be loyal and faithful to Him, even unto death. When we sometimes go astray, He has strange ways of calling us back to Him. And that is why we struggle with feelings of guilt, self-reproach and pain at times.

But God's heart is amazingly good as well. The moment that we reach out to Him, He is right there. As soon as we repent of our sin, He forgives. And the moment that we call out to Him, He helps us.

So be assured of this: God immediately forgives a child with a genuinely repentant heart. He promises in Isaiah 30:19: "You will weep no more. How gracious He will be when you cry for help! As soon as He hears, He will answer you."

God's forgiveness is complete and perfect.
Therefore, He will always pick fallen children back up.
Believe that and enjoy the feeling of relief it brings.

Thank You for accepting me unconditionally, time and again, and for always loving me. Amen.

JUNE 27

Become a Wholehearted Person

There is no condemnation for those who belong to Christ Jesus.
(Romans 8:1)

Dwight L. Moody said, "I have had more trouble with myself than with any other man." Does that sound like you? Yes, we women can mercilessly punish ourselves with feelings of self-reproach and guilt.

Days, months and even years after we made a mistake, we still walk around carrying a big bag of why-did-I-do-that? in our hearts. Long after God, and often the other person(s), have forgiven us, we still struggle to move on.

When God binds up our wounds of sin and guilt, He heals them completely. And therefore, He also wants you to forgive yourself one hundred percent. Yes, He wants you to be someone who has a heart that is whole so that you can truly live in the freedom to be found in Christ.

Don't dig up old wounds and don't dwell on the past. Allow God's grace to take them away completely and – this is important – forgive yourself wholeheartedly.

Through His redemptive act, God made His
children people who have whole hearts and can
face the future with confidence and live in freedom.
Know it. Believe it. And then live as a healed child.

Thank You for enabling me to live freely, dear Redeemer. Amen.

Keep on Praying

This is the confidence we have in approaching God: that if we ask anything according to His will: He hears us. (1 John 5:14)

Have there been times in your life that you felt like you were praying and praying, but that your prayers just had no effect at all; almost as if God did not hear them?

Yes, people do sometimes have to pray for months – even years – before they get an answer or a breakthrough. Sometimes God doesn't give us what we ask for. In times like these, it is easy to wonder: "Does He even hear me?" or "Why isn't He answering me?"

The answer is: He is always listening to all His children's hearts calling out to Him. He will never ever turn His back on us! However, God also knows when He should say "Yes!", when "No!" is more appropriate and when "Wait a bit, My child!" is in our best interest. We really can trust our Father with all our hearts.

God hears the prayers of every believer long before we even utter them. And He does indeed answer prayers! The answers may be unexpected and different from what we wanted, but still, He does answer!

Thank You for answering my prayers Your way and in Your time, faithful Father. Amen.

JUNE 29

Trust Him for a Breakthrough

You will weep no more. How gracious He will be when you cry for help! As soon as He hears, He will answer you. (Isaiah 30:19)

God is so faithful! I just realized this again the other day when He, in His typically unfathomable way, gave me an answer out of the blue.

I prayed about this one thing for years and I kept wondering why He wasn't giving a breakthrough, I begged and cried for Him to hear … and then, one day, God answered my prayer in the most unexpected way. He always provides answers and wisdom that amaze me! He really does make the impossible possible!

Dear friend, I can testify today; our God is faithful. He is amazingly wonderful. He is greater than great. And that is why His way of doing things and of answering prayers is just so incredibly surprising.

You just stay devoted to Him, devoted to your faith, to prayer, and to studying Scripture. Leave the rest up to Him as He knows exactly when to give you what.

I praise You for being so great and faithful, Father! And I know Your breakthrough is perfect! Amen.

Keep Blooming

And I am convinced that nothing can ever separate us from God's love. Neither death nor life, neither angels nor demons, neither our fears for today nor our worries about tomorrow – not even the powers of hell can separate us from God's love. (Romans 8:38)

None of us can, or will ever be able to, escape the pain in this world. And yet, children of God can live assured of the fact that nothing can happen to us without the Lord standing by us. Because He is always with us, even in the midst of our despair and brokenness, we are able to rise above circumstances that seem utterly hopeless.

For that reason, we don't find it strange that believers can smile through their tears and we also find that His children have the courage to bloom even in the most hostile of desert environments.

"No affliction nor temptation, no guilt nor power of sin, no wounded spirit nor terrified conscience should induce us to despair of help and comfort from God!" writes Thomas Scott.

May the Spirit make the seed of evergreen joy
sprout in your heart so that you can keep
blooming with a smile, even in times of drought.

In You, Lord, I find everlasting joy. Amen.

July

The Courage to Obey

*"We need only obey. There is guidance for each of us,
and by lowly listening we shall hear the right word."*

~ Ralph Waldo Emerson

"Return to Me, and I will return to you," says the Lord Almighty.

~ Malachi 3:7

Hear When He Speaks

There above it [the stairway to heaven] stood the LORD, and He said: "I am with you and will watch over you wherever you go …" (Genesis 28:13, 15)

You love the Lord and that is why you have a genuine desire to obey Him. Before we can obey Him, however, we must be willing to really listen for and hear God's voice. In order to hear Him, we need to listen very carefully as our Father has a way of speaking to His children in unexpected ways and places. And so:

- God sent Abraham an important message with three "ordinary" strangers (Gen. 18).
- God appeared to Jacob while he was asleep (Gen. 28:10-22).
- God regularly spoke to Joseph through various dreams (Gen. 41).
- Moses was called to perform the greatest task of his life by a voice from a burning bush (Exod. 3).
- Elijah heard God's command as a gentle whisper in the stillness (1 Kings 19:12).

Make sure that you are so tuned into God's voice that you are able to really hear Him speak in any place and in any manner.

Father God, please open my ears so that I can clearly hear Your voice. Amen.

Heed His Strange Commands

Then the LORD said to Abraham, "Why did Sarah laugh and say, 'Will I really have a child, now that I am old?' Is anything too hard for the LORD? I will return to you at the appointed time next year, and Sarah will have a son." (Genesis 18:13-14)

God not only speaks to His children in strange places and in strange ways, but quite often His message or command is also very strange. Time after time, His children are surprised at this strangeness:

- Just think how baffled Noah must have felt when he was told to build a 135-meter-long ship on dry ground.
- When God promised the 99-year-old Abraham and his 90-year-old wife that they would have a baby, it must have sounded impossible.
- And what a strange command did God give to Moses: to lead a nation of thousands of people through a desert without a definite route or proper provisions.

Noah did build the ark, Abraham was exactly 100 years old when his son, Isaac, was born and with God's help, Moses lead the Israelites safely through the desert for 40 years.

To God, the seemingly "impossible" commands are possible, because He is God. Believe that it is true for your life as well.

Thank You, Lord, that nothing is impossible with You. Amen.

Pass the Test

Then God said, "Take your son, your only son, whom you love – Isaac – and go to the region of Moriah. Sacrifice him there as a burnt offering on a mountain I will show you." (Genesis 22:2)

God's instructions can sometimes leave us stunned. How on earth could He expect Abraham to take his only son – the son that he had waited 100 years for – and tie him to an altar and then set him on fire? Wow!

Yes, God does sometimes ask people to do things that don't make any sense at first. And yet, God remains the God that always knows exactly what He is doing.

Abraham obeyed God every step of the way and God provided, unexpectedly and in the nick of time! "'Do not lay a hand on the boy,' He said. 'Do not do anything to him. Now I know that you fear God, because you have not withheld from Me your son, your only son'" (Gen. 22:12).

It may happen that God will also test you. He may ask you to do seemingly strange things and He may allow uncomfortable things to happen in your life to test your love for Him. What will you do with it?

Help me, great God, to obey You in all circumstances. Amen.

Remember That He Will Provide

[Abraham] went over and took the ram and sacrificed it as a burnt offering instead of his son. So Abraham called that place The LORD Will Provide. And to this day it is said, "On the mountain of the LORD it will be provided." (Genesis 22:13-14)

We serve a faithful and just God; a God that will look after His children and provide for their needs in all circumstances. Throughout history, we see how God provides believers with a way out, how He provides relief and how He provides for their needs in miraculous ways.

If you are unsure of whether your Father will meet all your specific needs, then know:

- God will never let one of His children down, including you.
- God provides answers in His special time and way; not yours.
- God's provision will be perfect and right on time – for your specific situation as well.

William Temple once said, "Every great person learns how to obey, who to obey, and when to obey."

Be patient if you have to wait on God's answer from time to time. The wait is quite often part of His perfect plan for your life.

Father of the Ages, thank You that I know I can trust You without reserve. Amen.

Enjoy His Blessing

The angel of the LORD called to Abraham from heaven a second time and said, "I swear by Myself, declares the LORD, that because you have done this and have not withheld your son, your only son, I will surely bless you." (Genesis 22:15-17)

God blesses obedience! And so God blessed Abraham for being faithful and obedient by making his descendants as numerous as the stars in the sky and as the sand on the seashore.

We would all like to enjoy God's blessing. After all, it is wonderful to have His love and approval, to receive guidance and wisdom from Him and to experience His awesome grace in our lives. How gloriously satisfying it is to be in His presence and experience His love when we have the boldness to appear before Him.

Yes, when we obey Him, His wonderful goodness is infinite. Remember Dietrich Bonhoeffer's words, "Only he who believes is obedient, and only he who is obedient believes."

Obedience, faith and God's goodness go together.
Make sure to enjoy His blessing every day by
faithfully and obediently following Him.

Lord, I really do want to obey You. Please help me to do so. Amen.

Bless Your Children's Children

"Abraham obeyed Me and did everything I required of him, keeping My commands, My decrees and My instructions." (Genesis 26:5)

Our faithful God has a way of spoiling His obedient children with im-measurable blessings. In biblical history, we can clearly see how faithful God was to, for instance, Abraham's descendants: Isaac, Jacob, Joseph, David and every single grandchild and even great-great-grandchild. God wrapped them all in His goodness. So therefore, it is evident that the Lord's blessing on His obedient children lasts for generations.

So, when you obey the commands of your Father, you are actually doing your descendants a favor. Not only do you teach them to live right by means of your example, but you also send God's goodness into the future with them.

And this blessing will not only envelop them here on earth, it will last for all eternity and follow them into the heavenly throne room.

Obedience has long-term benefits. Therefore,
pray that you will hear God's voice calling out
to you in all circumstances and ask for the
courage to hear and obey it faithfully.

Make me faithful – even unto death, O Lord. Amen.

Know That He Is with You

That night the LORD appeared to him and said, "I am the God of your father Abraham. Do not be afraid, for I am with you; I will bless you and will increase the number of your descendants for the sake of My servant Abraham." (Genesis 26:24)

We all fear someone or something at some point in our lives. We all feel unsure of ourselves when we are faced with a difficult task, when we must climb a high mountain, when we have to confront someone, when we need to settle an unpleasant matter or when we have to make a change.

If you find yourself at such a point in your life, then you can take what God said to Isaac to heart and make these words your own: "Do not be afraid, for I am with you." Can you hear it? Can you hear God reassuring you of His faithfulness and telling you that He will equip and strengthen you?

Remember, when you feel afraid and uncertain, God's power has the opportunity to become twice as strong while it is at work in you. You must just remain obedient. He is with you!

Thank You, great God, for never leaving me. Amen.

Be Sensitive for His Voice

Everyone who sins breaks the law; in fact, sin is lawlessness.
(1 John 3:4)

Have you ever wondered why you feel so guilty when you have done something wrong? Or when you just know that you were disobedient?

It is because, as a child of God, you have a wonderful gift. You have the Holy Spirit in you to prompt you and point you in the right direction. Because He shows you what is right and wrong deep down in your heart, you are automatically also more sensitive to the sin in your life. The closer you get to God, the more you read His Word and listen to His voice, the more aware you'll become of which road to take (and which road not to take).

The fact that you become more and more aware of your own disobedience and that you desire to follow His lead more and more is a good sign. Since that means you actually are hearing His voice.

Keep on listening to the whisper of the Holy Spirit in you
and then be courageous enough to obey Him. It is worth it!

Lord, I do want to hear You and do what You ask of me. Amen.

Don't Ignore His Voice

The Sovereign LORD has opened my ears; I have not been rebellious, I have not turned away. (Isaiah 50:5)

A pilot may be as experienced as they come, but if he ignores the instructions from the control tower, a disaster is inevitable. He may not be able to see the air traffic controller, but he can hear the person's voice and that is his only guide to a safe landing. So it is with God as well: whoever ignores His voice by being disobedient is heading for disaster.

Our Father does not necessarily speak to His children in a manner that is loud and clear. Quite often the whisper of His voice is nearly inaudible and His ways are almost invisible. And yet, it should not keep us from heeding His whisper and acting accordingly. When God whispers to us – either through His Spirit, His Word or other believers – He is serious about it.

May you, like Isaiah, say, "He wakens me morning by morning, wakens my ear to listen like one being instructed" (Isa. 50:4). The outcome of obeying God is ... a safe landing.

Help me to always be tuned into Your voice coming from the control tower of my life, Father. Amen.

Enjoy His Prosperity

"If you follow My decrees and are careful to obey My commands, I will send you rain in its season, and the ground will yield its crops and the trees their fruit." (Leviticus 26:3-4)

God will not let anyone mess with Him. Throughout the Word the message is clear: God blesses obedience and He punishes disobedience. We cannot expect to enjoy His goodness if we deliberately go against His will for us.

On the other hand, He promises us that He will reward His obedient children in His way and time. It is almost as if He treats them with extra care and compassion and wraps them in riches of peace.

For that reason, it is always worth it to try again – try to hear His voice again and then faithfully follow His commands. Like an anonymous writer once said, "Obeying God is always for our own good and for His glory."

There will always be a lot of rubbish on your life-path that will try to block the channel of communication between you and God. What you must do is to remain anchored in Him so that you will stay on course in the midst of it all. That is how to enjoy His prosperity.

Lord, today I want to live in Your holiness. Amen.

Resist the Evil One

"If in spite of this you still do not listen to Me but continue to be hostile toward Me then in My anger I will be hostile toward you, and I Myself will punish you for your sins seven times over."
(Leviticus 26:27-28)

God's love is infinite, unconditional and complete. He wants to wrap us in His love and spoil us with His blessings. But our Lord is also a jealous God that will not tolerate it if we trample on His love and goodness. He expects us to serve Him with all of our lives.

When we begin to understand something of His greatness and all-encompassing love, we will naturally desire to do His will. So if there is something in you that rebels against Him, it is time to search your heart. It may be that Satan is working very hard to steal you away from God. And that would be fatal!

Resist the powers of evil, fight against sin and
pray that God will hold you tightly every day.

Please forgive me for the times that I let You down, Lord. Make me faithful to the end. Amen.

Respect His Barricades

Then the LORD opened Balaam's eyes, and he saw the angel of the Lord standing in the road with his sword drawn. So he bowed low and fell facedown. (Numbers 22:31)

God wants you near Him at all times, because He wants to shower you with His grace and goodness. So, when you sometimes wander off or go off track, you should not be surprised if He uses unusual methods to get your attention and call you back to Him.

It was like that with Balaam, God's prophet, who had gone against God's will. In Numbers 22, we see that God clearly forbade Balaam to go with the leaders of Moab. But when Balaam disobeyed and went along with them, God placed an angel in the road to stop Balaam's donkey in its tracks. And then the angel explained to Balaam, "I have come here to oppose you because your path is a reckless one before Me" (Num. 22:32).

> Don't be surprised if God places a barrier in your way from time to time. Also, don't rebel when He wants you to let go of your own plans. It is God's way to protect you and to keep you close to Him.

Thank You for Your protection, Lord! Amen.

Do Exactly as He Says

But the Lord said to Moses and Aaron, "Because you did not trust in Me enough to honor Me as holy in the sight of the Israelites, you will not bring this community into the land I give them." (Numbers 20:12)

God's instructions to Moses were very clear. He was supposed to gather the people together, take the staff from the tabernacle and speak to the rock. Then God would let water flow forth from the rock to meet the needs of all the people.

But at this stage, Moses was sick and tired of the people's constant complaining on their journey through the desert. He allowed his impatience to get the better of him and so he didn't do exactly what God said.

Instead of speaking to the rock, he took the staff and struck the rock twice. As punishment for his disobedience, God did not allow Moses to enter the Promised Land.

Aren't we all guilty of twisting God's commands
just a little bit so they suit us better?

Forgive me for twisting Your truths to suit me, Lord! I want to obey You one hundred percent. Amen.

Speak from God's Mouth

"Well, I have come to you now," Balaam replied. "But I can't say what-
ever I please. I must speak only what God puts in my mouth."
(Numbers 22:38)

God sometimes asks us to do things that are not easy to do at all. Yes,
it may happen that He expects us to take a stand that goes against the
popular view on something, to deliver an unpleasant message or to go
and tell someone something that they are not going to like. The danger
here is that we may be tempted not to obey God's instruction.

And so it happened that God sent Balaam to deliver a strange
message to Balak. When Balak asked Balaam to say something else,
Balaam replied, "Did I not tell you I must do whatever the Lord says?"
(Num. 23:26).

"He that cannot obey, cannot command," said Benjamin Franklin.
Obedience means to listen carefully to God's voice and then
to do exactly as He says, even though it may be difficult.

Lord, please help me to fearlessly execute Your command and convey
Your message of truth. Amen.

Obey without Doubting

"And the LORD was also angry with me because of you. He said to me, 'Moses, not even you will enter the Promised Land!'"
(Deuteronomy 1:37)

Poor Moses! For 40 long years, he led the people through the wilderness, he listened to them complain and he interceded for them with God. And then … he was not allowed to enter into Canaan. Yes, sometimes it may seem as if God's punishment is just a little too harsh and then we may start doubting if He really is just.

The fact of the matter is that God is and stays God. And therefore, God can do as He pleases. So the next time that you start doubting God's way of doing things, just remember; God is good. He is great. And He is God! We are mere humans and we simply cannot comprehend Him and His ways.

What we are supposed to do is to trust Him and obey Him completely. John Climacus wrote, "Obedience is the burial of the will and the resurrection of humility."

When we obey our Father without doubting, then His grace has the opportunity to be fully at work in our lives. The grace that can unlock even "impossible" doors.

Lord, I may not always understand, but I always trust You. Amen.

Feel Welcome with God

This is how we know that we belong to the truth and how we set our hearts at rest in His presence: If our hearts condemn us, we know that God is greater than our hearts, and He knows everything.
(1 John 3:19-20)

Sin has a way of keeping us away from God. Just like Adam and Eve of old, we hide from Him when we know that we have done something wrong. Thank the Lord! He does not give up on us if we walk away, but always looks us up and calls us back to Him.

Know this today; God will never forsake you! Not even when you have committed sin and you feel guilty. No, that is actually when He is determined to find you, call you back to Him and welcome you with open arms. Just confess your wrongdoing to Him and be assured that He has already forgiven you.

"Dear friends, if our hearts do not condemn us,
we have confidence before God" (1 John 3:21).

Thank You, Lord, that I can know that You will always welcome me back. Amen.

Try Again

The one who does what is right is righteous, just as He is righteous.
The one who does what is sinful is of the devil. (1 John 3:7-8)

Do you also sometimes feel discouraged because you just can't seem to manage to always do God's will? I surely do.

How many times have we resolved to do something … and then we end up doing the exact opposite. It is just so easy to get impatient, to lose our temper or to be nasty to someone. And then you say in your heart, "Oh! Why can't I get it right to always behave like a child of God?"

The answer lies in the fact that we are, despite our very best intentions, only human. And for as long as we find ourselves in this broken world, we will not be perfect. The devil is simply too busy keeping us away from the truth.

God expects nothing more of us than to
keep on trying, to get back up when we fall
and to turn back if we have gone off track.

Holy God, please help me to try again and again. Amen.

Do Not Postpone

I am honored in the eyes of the LORD and my God has been my strength. (Isaiah 49:5)

"Postpone" is a word that often equals self-reproach and regret. The more we postpone what we are supposed to do, the harder it becomes and the worse we feel about ourselves. It is the same with obedience. When we know that we must do something, but we keep putting it off and coming up with excuses and saying that we, "will do it tomorrow", the failure to do it keeps preying on our conscience.

Since we are looking at obedience this month, God may have impressed a few things on you. Maybe there is someone that you need to forgive, something that you need to do for someone else, a lifestyle change that you need to make or a bad habit that you need to break. When you allow the Spirit to control you, He will work in you … until you obey.

> The peace you have in your heart is just too precious
> for it to be stolen by disobedience. So, take the bull
> by the horns today and do what you know you must.

Holy Spirit, give me the courage to be faithful to You without reserve, from today onwards. Amen.

Stay in God's Family

The one who keeps God's commands lives in Him, and He in them. And this is how we know that He lives in us: We know it by the Spirit He gave us. (1 John 3:24)

Isn't God incredibly good to us? To think that He considers us part of His family – His inner circle! We are not only His children, but also His brothers and sisters.

The fact that we are part of God's family tree means that we are working together for the same cause – just like in any other family business. It means that we are all striving towards the same goal: We want to do His will and we want to be like Him.

Fortunately, our dear Father does not leave us to look after His interests by ourselves. No, He gives us the Holy Spirit to help us with it every day.

You never have to look after God's interests all on your own. The Holy Spirit is working alongside you and equips you to do God's will every day. Just trust Him with it.

Thank You that I can be part of your holy family, Father God. Make me a loyal family member. Amen.

Be Renewed Every Day

Do not conform to the pattern of this world, but be transformed by the renewing of your mind. Then you will be able to test and approve what God's will is – His good, pleasing and perfect will. (Romans 12:2)

Faith starts from scratch every single day. We cannot live today on yesterday's faith. Yesterday is over. There is only one way to stay in God's will and that is to declare our faith in Him and our obedience to Him anew every day. Then, says Paul, we will know what He expects of us in every circumstance.

Allow the Holy Spirit to renew you every day at the break of dawn. Declare your dependence on Him and ask Him to help you with every aspect of your life in particular. Pray about your plans for the day, the tasks that you have to perform, the people who you will meet and the roads that you will travel on.

Give your life – your entire life – to Him with hope and then know: His mercies are also brand new every morning!

Thank You, dear Spirit of God, for starting over with me every day. Amen.

Show New Love

Dear friends, since God so loved us, we also ought to love one another. No one has ever seen God; but if we love one another, God lives in us and His love is made complete in us. (1 John 4:11-12)

Do you think that other people can see that you are a member of God's family? Do your words and actions convey to others that He is living in you?

If you have genuine love for others and if you express it, then your answer to these questions would be "yes". Because God is love. And God's love should be engraved in every single aspect of His children's lives. His love must be audible, visible and tangible in our lives.

Start every day with new love; love that forgives completely, accepts unconditionally and that involves self-sacrifice – regardless of what may have happened yesterday. Because then you will be putting the truth of God-is-love into practice in your life.

"The fruit of the Spirit grows only in the garden of obedience," said Terry Fulham. Treat others in such a way that they will know that your love is new every day – just like Christ's.

Father, today I want to live out Your love. Please help me to do that. Amen.

Live Out Creative Love

And so we know and rely on the love God has for us. God is love.
Whoever lives in love lives in God, and God in them. (1 John 4:16)

New love is creative. Just think of how young couples that are in love come up with creative plans to impress one another and to declare their love. There seems to be no end to their vocabulary of love, their acts of love and the ways in which they express their love.

If it is our heart's desire to visibly live out God's love, we will not find it hard to think of new, creative ways to show love. When we want to love like He does:

- we will have understanding and sympathy for others;
- we will have compassion for others and we will reach out to them;
- we will take note of other people's needs and then do something about it; and
- we will be different, we will speak and act like Christ.

Think of new ways to show love every morning. Make an effort to make the everyday unexpectedly pleasant for others by spontaneously living out His love. It is a nice way to be obedient.

Loving Father, how, where and with whom can I share Your love today?
Amen.

Live Out True Family Love

Love must be sincere. Hate what is evil; cling to what is good. Be devoted to one another in love. Honor one another above yourselves. (Romans 12:9-10)

We have the privilege of being part of a family so that we can express love towards others. However, we also know for a fact that we're not all crazy about one another just because we are related. On the contrary, there is usually a lot more strife and disharmony to be found in family circles.

Romans 12:9-21 is meant for the Christ family. It is very straight forward in giving us various instructions for how we are supposed to care for one another. It makes it very clear that the password for any healthy relationship is love: Love that lives in peace and harmony with others, love that is humble and not selfish, love that treats others with respect.

Take this passage from Scripture and put it up on a wall somewhere where you can see it. Read through it every time that you feel irritated or angry with someone, or when you have had enough of the "nonsense" of the world.

Live love-in-action. Action that shows you care.

Lord, please engrave Your prescripts for love deep in my heart. Amen.

JULY 24

Love-In-Action

Be careful to do what is right in the eyes of everyone. (Romans 12:17)

If we truly want to obey God's command to love, we cannot be passive about it. Because true love requires us to take action. Love:

- makes you treat others with respect;
- makes you help people who are suffering;
- opens your purse, hands and heart to others;
- teaches you to treat your enemies well;
- will let you make time for others;
- will let you forget about yourself and your own interests; and
- leaves hate and revenge in God's hands.

It is not always easy to implement love-in-action. But it is a command that we must try our hardest to obey every day of our lives. In fact, God wants us to showcase His great love to the world by living this way.

Let's pray and ask the Holy Spirit every day to give
us the courage to visibly live out His kind of love.

Heavenly God, there is no way that I can love like You want me to in my own strength. But thank You that I am indeed able to do it with Your help. Amen.

Be Debt-Free

Let no debt remain outstanding, except the continuing debt to love one another, for whoever loves others has fulfilled the law.
(Romans 13:8)

Debt has a nasty way of catching up on us. And it is not nice to think that you owe someone something. However, love also has a way of being interest bearing. When we have enough love in our hearts and we regularly make love deposits in other people's lives, their love accounts will be full. But, if we keep withdrawing from these accounts with loveless words and actions, we will eventually empty out our own as well as other people's hearts and we will literally be left bankrupt.

How much love do you deposit in the hearts of the people around you every day? Do you make frequent deposits or do you only withdraw from their love accounts? Take time today and make a list of all your relationships and then write down the percentage of love that you add to each person's life. Be sure to make large deposits into the love accounts of all your relationships over the next few days. And where you are in debt … go donate love, in excess!

Pray that you will live out God's command to fully love every day.

Help me to love like You do, Master of Love. Amen.

Live by the Spirit

But you, dear friends, by building yourselves up in your most holy faith and praying in the Holy Spirit. (Jude verse 20)

We live in a time when the Gospel is often under attack. Millions of people just cannot imagine or believe that Jesus Christ is the Son of God and that we can have eternal life through faith in Him. The fact of the matter is that throughout all the ages, the world will question and doubt the message of Christ.

Therefore Jude, one of Jesus' earthly brothers, warns believers against false teachers. Jude says that to stay on the right faith track, we must ensure that our faith becomes stronger every day, we must build our lives on God and we must allow the Holy Spirit to work through us.

Dear fellow believer, don't allow Satan to draw you away from God with all kinds of clever-sounding arguments. God is God and Christ is your Redeemer. Pray and ask the Holy Spirit to strengthen you in your faith in Him and obedience to Him again today.

Lord Jesus, help me to faithfully follow You – no matter what. Amen.

JULY 27

Stay in God's Protection

Keep yourselves in God's love as you wait for the mercy of our Lord Jesus Christ to bring you to eternal life. (Jude verse 21)

God will never leave His children alone in this world. Like a faithful Father, He builds a strong wall of protection around each of us. We are wrapped in His goodness so that we can feel safe and secure. This wall of grace is also there to protect us against the world's waves of doubt, unchristian attacks and non-biblical statements.

When you doubt God's goodness, it is important to realize that God's faithfulness to you is steadfast; He watches over you and guards you like a jealous Father. On top of that, He also made sure that there are other believers with you within these walls-of-goodness.

These people are there to encourage you, specifically in times of doubt. When you feel insecure, reach out to other believers – they are there to offer you helping hands and faithful prayers.

Regularly pray for and with other children
of God. It will help you to remember that
His steadfast love always watches over you.

Thank You, Master, for protecting me in so many ways! Amen.

Hold Onto Other Believers

Be merciful to those who doubt. (Jude verse 22)

Continually living according to God's will is certainly not easy. And to always have a strong faith is also difficult for us humans. Every day, there are literally thousands of things, people and circumstances that all compete for our attention. And for that reason, believers desperately need one another.

Ecclesiastes 4:9-10 explains it very well, "Two are better than one, because they have a good return for their labor: If either of them falls down, one can help the other up."

Dear fellow pilgrim, don't try to undertake your journey of faith all on your own. Make sure to surround yourself with fellow believers. Hold each other's hands in faith, pray for one another, enjoy reading the Word together and talk about your journey of faith.

Hold onto your friends who believe in God. Because
when you fall, the others will be there to pick
you up and get you back on track.

Lord, help me to obey Your command to be part of a community of believers. Amen.

JULY 29

Play in His Symphony

… so that with one mind and one voice you may glorify the God and Father of our Lord Jesus Christ. (Romans 15:6)

You are part of God's great symphony! And you can relax … this orchestra has nothing to do with your musical talents or abilities! It is all about the song of love in your heart. As a child of God, your life is an instrument that plays in God's symphony of love every day. When your heart is tuned into God, your life will automatically make the most beautiful sounds. When you are tuned into His voice and the needs of those around you, there will be peace and harmony in your life.

When your life brings forth notes that are out of tune and you can't bear to listen to that particular piece of music, it is important to search your own heart. In such times, you must allow Him to once again tune in your heart by removing all the impure notes from it so that you can be in harmony with Him again.

Now, allow His peace and love to wash over you in your quiet time so that your life will harmonize perfectly today.

Holy Spirit, tune my life into Your will, please. Amen.

Have Obedient Hope

May the God of hope fill you with all joy and peace as you trust in Him, so that you may overflow with hope by the power of the Holy Spirit. (Romans 15:13)

Disobedience to God has a way of knocking us down. Yes, sin crushes us. So in times when you don't feel competent to be a child of God because of your disobedience, all joy vanishes from your life. No one can be part of the destruction without also being sucked in and pulled down by it.

The best way to get out of this phase-of-falling is to genuinely repent as soon as possible and to receive God's forgiveness. When you do that, you will see His outstretched hand reaching to pick you back up and hold you to His chest.

Today and every day of your life, hold onto the promise that God will fully forgive you if you repent in all sincerity. And then live with abundant hope and joy!

Thank You, Lord, that I have yet another chance to try and be Your obedient child. Amen.

He Is Waiting for You

To Him who is able to keep you from stumbling and to present you before His glorious presence without fault and with great joy.
(Jude verse 24)

You have just let out your last breath. In an instant you are surrounded by white light that carries you away. You look down on your earthly body and you see the people mourning your passing, but none of it matters anymore. All you want to do is to get to God. You turn away from the earthly scene and you let yourself be engulfed by the white light … and then … you are with the Holy One.

You feel how He fills your entire being and His glory overwhelms you. For the very first time you truly comprehend the full impact of what the word "grace" means. You spontaneously start to sing along with the other believers as they praise and worship Him. And you think: *How great is our God …*

> God is already waiting for you at the gates of heaven.
> And while you are still on earth, He is with you
> every step of the way. What a great God He is!

Holy Lord, I want to obey You and follow You faithfully to the end of my life. Amen.

August

The Courage to Be Happy

"Until you make peace with who you are,
you'll never be content with what you have."

~ Doris Mortman

With joy you will draw water from the wells of salvation.

~ Isaiah 12:3

A Renewed Heart

*Bring joy to Your servant, L*ORD*, for I put my trust in You.*
(Psalm 86:4)

Have you also noticed that humankind seems to suffer greatly from a condition called discontentment? Is seems like no one is able to be happy and content. Recent research found that the level of happiness for people living in developed countries has dropped to the lowest point ever. It seems as if the more people have, the less they are able to find true happiness.

William Barclay writes that there are so many children of God that have either lost their joy or never knew joy in the first place; that have become joyless Christians; that no longer know of the freedom that resonates in the depths of a believer's heart.

Let's resolve to start thinking differently about things this month, to ban all the *un*-things from our lives; be it unhappiness, unrest or feeling unsatisfied.

Let's pray and ask the Holy Spirit to renew our hearts
and fill them with true happiness and abundant joy.

Teach me the truths of joy, please Lord. Amen.

Live in His Strength

The way of the LORD is a refuge for the blameless, but it is the ruin of those who do evil. (Proverbs 10:29)

It is terrible to feel like we can't get something right, or that everything we start ends up being a failure, or that we will never be successful and happy. It is particularly hard when we look at other people who seem to have it all – their lives are perfect and always full of joy.

The truth, however, is that no one's life is perfect. Every single person has experienced pain or failure or has something that upsets them or makes them unhappy. Happy people are the ones that have learnt to rise above their circumstances, to look past the discomfort and to find the positive in every situation.

They have gone through difficult times that taught them to hold on to the hope of a better tomorrow. And maybe happy people have made peace with the fact that no one will ever be able to do everything right and that failure is not the end of the world.

Pray and ask the Holy Spirit to let the seed of heavenly joy germinate deep in your inner being. Let the fact that you are His child be the compost that will help the seed of joy grow.

Make me strong, full of faith and happy, Father. Amen.

Discover Joy

I said to myself, "Come now, I will test you with pleasure to find out what is good." (Ecclesiastes 2:1)

Humankind is always looking for happiness. Every person on earth desires it, actively pursues it and tries to find it. But very few do!

Why? Is it because we don't really know what happiness is? Because we have never defined it for ourselves in our own words? Or because we are looking for it in the wrong places and in the wrong way?

Ask the people around you what would make them happy and you will probably get answers like the following; to be rich so I never have to worry about money, to be successful and to perform well, to be famous and admired by others … Here and there, you may also get answers like these; to be healthy, to be happily married, to have my children be happy or to have loyal friends.

Very few people will say a happy life is to do God's will.

Start this discover-joy-month by taking a few days and reflecting on what true, lasting joy in life really means to you. Ask the Holy Spirit to reveal it to you – He will!

Holy Spirit, will You please share the secret of heavenly joy with me? Amen.

Evaluate the Joys of the World

Do not wear yourself out to get rich; do not trust your own cleverness. Cast but a glance at riches, and they are gone, for they will surely sprout wings and fly off to the sky like an eagle. (Proverbs 23:4-5)

If happiness equals wealth, status, fame and achievements, then why are there so many people in the world that have all these things … and yet they are still unhappy? How can people make stacks of money and still not be content with what they have? Why are there so many celebrities in Hollywood that need antidepressants or other drugs just to make it through the day? And what is the reason for the broken relationships in the lives of so many successful people?

The world's way to measure happiness is totally distorted and so we should look for the answers in Scripture. Happiness cannot be found in earthly accomplishments. On the contrary, earthly success quite often leads to unhappy hearts and can also disappear in the blink of an eye.

There is only one place where you can find lasting joy: in the center of your heart. There where you have fellowship with your Father!

Lord, please remove the desire for earthly "happiness" from my heart so that I can find true joy with You! Amen.

Invite Happiness into Your Heart

They seldom reflect on the days of their life, because God keeps them occupied with gladness of heart. (Ecclesiastes 5:20)

Do you really want to be happy? Now you're probably wondering: what kind of a question is that? Of course I do! But think about this again: do you really want to see yourself being someone who is happy with life?

Or is there a part of you that still feeds on the unhappiness in your life, on the drama of everything that is wrong and on the sympathy that the world offers you when you are unhappy? If there is a part of you that is gratified by all the unhappiness in your life, then you will certainly attract more unhappiness to yourself.

For that reason, you must have a deep-rooted heart's desire for happiness to be a happy person – to be someone who chooses to be happy with life and who pursues and expresses joy every day.

Ask yourself: Do I really want to be happy? Ask the Spirit to give you that deep yearning for true happiness, ask Him to remove the things that block the flow of joy in your heart and to help you receive life-changing joy.

Father God, please empty me of myself and fill me with You. Make me full of Your joy. Amen.

The Courage to Be Daring

I rejoice in following Your statutes as one rejoices in great riches.
(Psalm 119:14)

Are you afraid of saying "yes" to happiness? Afraid that it might disappoint you, that it might cause you to feel uncomfortable or that it might be taken away from you? Maybe you were once ecstatic about something in the past, but then the feeling gave way to something quite the opposite soon after that. And so now you have closed your heart to happiness.

For as long as we live on earth and we have to deal with the reality of life, the chances are that we will feel disenchanted from time to time. However, our being happiness-unfit, should not keep us from exercising our happiness muscles so as to master the art of being happy. Barbara Johnson said to practice finding joy and you will be surprised at where you find it.

> Don't allow cynicism to steal your desire for true happiness. Dare to be truly happy (again). Look for happiness in the right places. And live it!

Lord, I know You want to see me happy. Give my heart the courage to be happy. Amen.

Choose to Be Happy

He will yet fill your mouth with laughter and your lips with shouts of joy. (Job 8:21)

Did you know that being happy is a choice? That you do have the ability to be a happy person – regardless of your circumstances? You really can control your own happiness, because joy does not depend on external factors, it comes from deep within yourself.

A study that looked at 22 people who had won the lottery and 22 people leading normal lives, found that over time the lottery winners were not at all happier than the losers were. So, money could not buy happiness. Likewise, it is thought that people in high positions, celebrities and the so-called stars are not necessarily happier than the 8-5 office worker or your average Joe. Happy people are found everywhere … because they are the ones who made the right choice.

There is joy when we look at the past, there is joy in the present and there is joy when we look to the future.

People that are happy with their lives are people who decided to be happy – no matter what. And that is why they bloom with joy. Have you made the decision to be happy?

God of joy, today I choose to be happy. I choose You! Amen.

Seek Eternal Pleasures

The fear of the LORD is the beginning of knowledge, but fools despise wisdom and instruction. (Proverbs 1:7)

Short-lived worldly happiness and pleasure are very much like a big slab of chocolate. You crave it, bite into it and devour it within a few short minutes … but then you still feel hungry. On top of that, you also feel bad and fairly guilty afterwards as well!

There is but one lasting solution if we have a genuine desire for deep-rooted fulfillment. We have to swap fleeting pleasures for a deep, personal relationship with our heavenly Father. Only He can fill our empty hearts with permanent joy. Only He can satisfy our hungry souls and only He has the ability to give us true and lasting happiness.

Don't waste your life on short-lived, fleeting pleasures that give you nothing but a headache anyway. What Solomon says is true: Doing that is pure foolishness! Allow the Holy Spirit to fill your heart with peace and joy that will last forever.

Father, I want to be eternally happy. Yes, I do want to experience Your kind of happiness every day. Please show me how. Amen.

Live Freely

Not only is this so, but we also boast in God through our Lord Jesus Christ, through whom we have now received reconciliation.
(Romans 5:11)

We so often live a life burdened by our own weaknesses, sin and limitations. Yes, as women we tend to blame and criticize ourselves for what we are doing, or not doing, for who we are, or for who we are not … while we could actually be living as joyful children of the Most High every day!

Children that are happy because Christ has already done everything to make sure that we are free – despite our brokenness – and because we are heavenly children that will one day stand before His throne.

Don't keep thinking of yourself as God's problem child. Christ is not disappointed in you. He is just busy helping you to become more and more like Him every day. So, when He points out to you that you could have done something differently, He is merely making you stronger and better.

You are free! Believe it! So, go and live every day like a free child who has thousands of reasons to celebrate.

Thank You, Savior God, that I can find true happiness through You and with You. Amen.

Live a Meaningful Life

When Jesus spoke again to the people, He said, "I am the light of the world. Whoever follows Me will never walk in darkness, but will have the light of life." (John 8:12)

When you sometimes feel a little discouraged, do you ever wonder if life is worth it? If there is any point to your daily routine and existence?

Yes, from time to time, we all grapple with questions about life, the meaning of it all and hope for the future. Now, Jesus tells us that His children have no reason to feel like this, because He declares that those who follow Him will live a meaningful life and they will also have light so that they can see what they need to do to please God (verse 12).

Jesus makes it very clear that the people who have a personal relationship with Him and that strive to do His will, will surely receive His light: the light that gives their lives meaning.

> When you build your life on the Rock, seek His will
> and do it and strive to glorify Him with your life, then
> your life will be filled with meaning and happiness.

Let Your light of life shine through me today, heavenly God. I do want to follow it. Amen.

Live with Joy

Blessed are those who find wisdom, those who gain understanding.
(Proverbs 3:13)

Solomon's Proverbs is a book full of wisdom for happiness and in it he tells us again and again why we can experience joy when living as children of God:

- The Omniscient One is our God and we love Him. Therefore, He accompanies us day after day. "The fear of the LORD is the beginning of wisdom, and knowledge of the Holy One is understanding" (Prov. 9:10).
- We have the Spirit of God to guide us in the truth of life every day. "The mocker seeks wisdom and finds none, but knowledge comes easily to the discerning" (Prov. 14:6).
- Through the Spirit, we are able to live a life that makes a difference in the world around us. "The words of the mouth are deep waters, but the fountain of wisdom is a rushing stream" (Prov. 18:4).

All wisdom and happiness start with love for the Lord,
or fear of the Lord as the Bible puts it. The lives of those
that love Him and obey Him are full of pure joy.

Thank You that I know a life with You is filled with meaning and joy.
Amen.

Live with Gratitude

"Those who sacrifice thank offerings honor Me, and to the blameless I will show My salvation." (Psalm 50:23)

It doesn't matter how critical a situation may seem or how many reasons we may have to feel unhappy and worried, the moment that we start to thank and praise our Father, our hearts change. When we worship Him, it is as if peace and joy just wash over us and it makes the darkness disappear. Because God has a way of blessing His children that gratefully exalt Him with unfathomable peace.

Try to start every morning with a prayer of thanksgiving. Keep your eyes and heart focused on what you can be grateful for throughout the day and then go to bed with a worshipful prayer on your lips.

Then you will find that your Father helps you in ways you could never even have imagined, that He gives you breakthroughs when you least expect it and that He strengthens you particularly in the times that you feel vulnerable and weak.

Today, remember the words by Jim Beggs:
"This day and your life are God's gift to you:
so give thanks and be joyful always!"

I praise, honor and thank You, great God. Amen.

Joy in Your Heart

Worship the LORD with gladness; come before Him with joyful songs. Know that the LORD is God. (Psalm 100:2-3)

There are millions of reasons for people to be unhappy. Pain, disease, death, rejection, molestation, financial distress and poverty in no way contribute to our level of happiness. And yes, this old life certainly is no fairy tale where people "live happily ever after".

In the face of all the reasons for unhappiness, children of the Living God, however, have something that sets them apart from those that are unsaved. We live our lives knowing that we are saved and that we can therefore look forward to a glorious life with our God.

We also live with the knowledge that we are never alone, not one moment of our lives, because the Holy Spirit is our Standby who wraps us in grace and guides and carries us through everything.

Billy Graham once said that the fact that grace is undeserved makes Christians the only people on earth that always have something to be happy about. Do you have *joie de vivre?*

Thank You, Master of life, that through and in You I can have joy in my heart. Amen.

Take Him at His Word

Let us hold unswervingly to the hope we profess, for He who promised is faithful. (Hebrews 10:23)

People disappoint us, frustrate us and have the ability to sometimes make us feel sad right down to our souls. This is because people break their promises, change over time and often don't understand us. Fortunately, we don't have to rely on people alone and our joy does not depend on them either, because we have something else. Since we know Christ, we have all the infallible promises in His Word to rely on:

- "The Lord is my light and my salvation – whom shall I fear? For in the day of trouble He will keep me safe in His dwelling" (Ps. 27:1, 5).
- "'I have seen their ways, but I will heal them; I will guide them and restore comfort to Israel's mourners, creating praise on their lips. Peace, peace, to those far and near,' says the Lord. 'And I will heal them'" (Isa. 57:18-19).
- "And hope does not put us to shame, because God's love has been poured out into our hearts through the Holy Spirit, who has been given to us" (Rom. 5:5).
- We have an Advocate with the Father – Jesus Christ, the Righteous One. He is the atoning sacrifice for our sins …" (1 John 2:1-2).

How lucky are we that we have God, in
whose Word we put our faith and trust!

Lord, thank You for understanding me and always being reliable. Amen.

See Clearly Again

For God, who said, "Let light shine out of darkness" ...
(2 Corinthians 4:6)

Many of us have gone stark blind. We are so used to being able to see and we are so bored with the things that we see, that we have become completely blind to it all.

When was the last time that you silently sat and watched a bird, that you really took in the sunrise or sunset, that you looked intently at your loved ones' faces or that you admired the beauty of your own body? Do you see God in your daily life? Do you really notice the beauty of nature, the valuable pearls of wisdom in His Word, the way He works in people, the miracles that He does in your life as well as in the lives of others and the way He protects you?

Billy Sunday said that, "if you have no joy in your religion, there's a leak in your Christianity somewhere."

Dear friends, let's take the time once again
to truly notice the wonder of life. When we are
able to truly see, we'll be able to truly live again.
Go through life with your eyes wide open.

Dear God, please take away my human blindness so that I can see Your light in my life once again. Amen.

Speak the Language of Love

The mouth of the righteous is a fountain of life ... [and] love covers over all wrongs. (Proverbs 10:11-12)

The way we live quite often determines our happiness. The way we treat other people, how we talk to them and the patience and compassion we show them generally adds to our own sense of self-worth, our self-image and ultimately our happiness.

As believers, we are specially equipped to treat others with dignity and love. After all, we have the Holy Spirit in us; the Spirit that will guide us to behave in the right way.

Do you think your words mean anything to others? Do you contribute to their system of values and do you think that you are making a positive impact on their lives? As from today, try your very best to be a source of inspiration to others; try to have constructive conversations and try to love and accept people the way that God does.

Happiness often depends on the words we say to and about others. How happy do you make other people? And how happy are you?

Father of Grace, please teach me the ABCs of Your language of love. Amen.

Walk in His Grace

"If you keep My commands, you will remain in My love, just as I have kept My Father's commands and remain in His love." (John 15:10)

The will of God will never take you where the grace of God cannot keep you. And don't we know it! How many times have we experienced the greatness of God's grace in our lives?

Those times when everything seemed hopeless and He gave us a miraculous breakthrough; when we were heartbroken because of broken relationships, He healed our hearts and when everything seemed to be going wrong, He brought it all back on track. Yes, even when we were lost in sin, His love set us free.

Live today knowing that your Father's grace will be sufficient for you and that He will carry you through this day too – just like He did in the past. Find joy in the knowledge that He will carry you through everything that could ever happen to you!

Help me, Lord, to live every moment with You. Amen.

Grow through Him

But when He, the Spirit of truth, comes, He will guide you into all the truth. (John 16:13)

God is constantly busy working in you! Like a gardener, He takes the weeds out of your heart on a daily basis and He works compost into the soil of your life so that you can grow and become stronger.

Furthermore, He waters you with the power of His Word so that you can have joy in life. Yes, God is working in you because He wants you to be molded into His image more and more every day.

- Be grateful for the times when you have a guilty conscience. That is a sign that God is busy pulling out the weeds of sin.
- Be glad when you grow your faith – that is the Spirit helping you to develop a stronger connection with Him.
- Be overjoyed when you succeed in applying the wisdom of His Word to your life.

> Just like you can't observe a tree growing, you also can't observe your own growth towards God.

Thank You for tending to my soul day after day, Father. Amen.

Remember: He Is on His Way!

He who testifies to these things says, "Yes, I am coming soon." Amen. Come, Lord Jesus. (Revelation 22:20)

While we are busy with our daily routine and trying our best to keep our earthly tent standing, it is very easy to forget that we are moving one day closer to our Lord Jesus' return and our heavenly home every single day. We are moving closer to the place where we will experience glorious joy for evermore!

Don't let the pressures of this world, doing your daily stint and all your responsibilities make you lose perspective. Remember that this earthly life is very short and only temporary. For that reason, keep praying and asking the Holy Spirit to help you live a balanced life – a life in which you enjoy your time on earth while you prepare for your heavenly home.

Ask Him to show you how and where you need to adjust the rhythm of your life so that you can be in step with Him in order to be ready when He comes.

Your Father is on His way! Therefore, live this day with a heart that clings to Him and that is thus filled with joy.

Lord, teach me to pay as much attention to my life-one-day as I do to my life-right-now. Amen.

Share Your Fountain of Joy

Praise the LORD. Blessed are those who fear the LORD, who find great delight in His commands. (Psalm 112:1)

The celebrated author, Pascal, once said that "happiness can be found neither in ourselves nor in external things, but in God …" The fountain and true source of happiness is found in a life that is in right standing with God – and therefore, also in right standing with other people.

When God is your alpha and omega, when you know how much you need Him and when you draw strength from His love every day, then there is already a fountain of joy in your life. And because the source of this fountain is true and right, other wonderful joys flow forth from it as well; delights like healthy relationships, the giving and receiving of love, job satisfaction and peace and rest for your soul.

On top of that, His Spirit enables you to share some of the glory of God with others.

Is the Fountain of Life flowing through you?

Spirit of God, bubble up in me today, fill me up and then flood my banks with Your living and soul-quenching water. Amen.

AUGUST 21

Find Joy in the Mundane

Sacrifice thank offerings to God, fulfill Your vows to the Most High.
(Psalm 50:14)

How can ordinary people with a normal lifestyle attain above-average levels of happiness?

Such people must have found the secret to happiness … and it is living a grateful life. They find something to be grateful for in everything. And that is why they are always filled with joy.

Maybe one of the obstacles in the road to happiness is the fact that humankind so quickly and easily takes people and things for granted. The situation or person that initially gave us great joy, soon becomes something that we have gotten used to.

On the other hand, happy people have learnt never to take anything or anyone for granted, but to be genuinely grateful for everything in their lives. That is why they are able to find joy in ordinary, everyday life and why they rejoice over everyone they get to share their lives with.

Pray that the Holy Spirit will once again open your
eyes to the miracles that are to be found in every
day, the people who God placed around you and
every little undeserved joy that comes your way.

Today I realize that I have lost the art of being genuinely grateful. Open my heart once again, please Lord. Amen.

Be Successful

Give careful thought to the paths for your feet and be steadfast in all your ways. (Proverbs 4:26)

Happiness results in success. Not the other way around! A study that focused on employees found that happy people more readily received salary increases and promotions and consequently moved up the ladder of success faster. Their attitude towards work naturally lead to their success. Just like fame and money, our job per se cannot make us happy. Rather, it is our attitude towards our job and work that makes all the difference.

Do you see your job as something that you have to do and that you just want to be over and done with as soon as possible? Do Monday mornings cause you to sink into depression and do you hold your breath for Friday afternoons? Or do you find fulfillment in your job because you see the bigger picture and because you know that you are making a difference? If that is the case, then you will be happy and therefore you will also be successful.

Try to see your job in a different light today.
Try helping others while you are doing your job.

Holy Leader, help me to have the right attitude towards my job please. Amen.

Remember What You Have

The house of the righteous contains great treasure, but the income of the wicked brings ruin. (Proverbs 15:6)

People have a natural tendency to always be aware of those things that they don't have. We are bombarded with advertisements that tell us that we simply have to have this or that product. We compare ourselves to others and then think how little we have. We strive for more, even more, bigger and better … in the hope of one day finding happiness.

And yet we stay unsatisfied in our desire for more of the world. We are so focused on the things that we want to and have to get a hold of, that we completely forget about the people who we already have all around us. It happens much too often that we only realize how much someone means to us the day that they are no longer there.

Take some time today to make a list of all the people in your life that have made a difference in your life, that make your life easier and everyone who loves you and cares for you. Think of them often and tell them how much they mean to you.

Today, remember who you have in your life and you'll be surprised at how lucky (and happy!) you really are.

Thank You, God of joy, for every single person in my life – I treasure them. Amen.

Have the Right Attitude

A heart at peace gives life to the body. (Proverbs 14:30)

"There is little difference in people, but that little difference makes a big difference. The little difference is attitude. The big difference is whether it is positive or negative." This is what Clement Stone had to say concerning the importance of your heart's attitude.

Are you also one of those people who allow the smallest things to get you down or make you sick with worry; someone who is generally negative and who easily falls into depression? Or are you one of those always-smiling people who see the light in any circumstance and can find joy in any situation?

We don't always have control over the things that come our way. We can also not manage other people's attitudes and behavior towards us. We can, however, ask the Holy Spirit to give us a heart filled with hope and optimism. Because even a small piece of positive joy can transform the most critical situation into something different.

> Today, maintain a positive and constructive attitude
> towards every single aspect of your life. After all, you
> can handle everything with God by your side.

Thank You for being my Father and my God through thick and thin. Amen.

Be Content with What You Have

*Honor the LORD with your wealth, with the firstfruits of all your crops;
then your barns will be filled to overflowing, and your vats will brim
over with new wine. (Proverbs 3:9-10)*

Happy people are content people. They are people who have made peace with a lot of things: With their strengths as well as with their weaknesses, with what they have and with what they will never have. They don't rebel against the things that they can do nothing about, but they take responsibility for those things that they can indeed manage.

Happy people don't sit around waiting for others to make their hearts happy, no, they find that deep-rooted joy within themselves and then they share it with everyone around them.

Yes, people who have discovered the secret to happiness have learnt that no person, possession, riches or achievements can make a permanent difference to how happy their hearts feel.

They know that you can only be truly happy by being satisfied with doing God's will.

Happiness is to need nothing more, because you already
have everything you need ... because you have Christ.

Heavenly Father, thank You that I already have everything I need. Amen.

AUGUST 26

Sow Happiness

Better a small serving of vegetables with love than a fattened calf with hatred. (Proverbs 15:17)

You can change the world – if you are happy!

Do you know what happens once you have made the decision to be happy? You think differently, you even look and act differently. Because then you are content with your circumstances. And because you are someone who is content, you think positively about your life, your job and the people around you. Then everything about you is totally different, your words, your facial expression and the way you act.

The wonder of life is that when you sow good things, you will also attract good things to you. The harvest that you reap is often equal to what you have worked into the soil of your life. But even more than that, your happiness is contagious and others will "catch" it. You will change the attitudes and mindsets of the people around you because you radiate positive energy and you share the joy of living.

Decide to sow happiness today. You will find
that a great measure of the good that you sow
will also fall on the soil of your own heart.

Guide of my life, teach me the art of planting flowers of joy in other people's lives. Amen.

Fly His Flag

Surely God is my salvation; I will trust and not be afraid. The LORD, the LORD Himself, is my strength and my defense; He has become my salvation. (Isaiah 12:2)

For as long as we are on earth, the chambers of our hearts will need maintenance work. There may even come times when it feels like our lives are crumbling and falling to pieces.

However, when we have the King in our hearts, we live lives that are – despite everything – different. Because we know that we are children of grace: Children that are blessed, in any and all circumstances, with the presence and abundance of God.

When you sometimes feel like your world is falling apart, then you need to remind yourself that your Father is in control and that you are a chosen child of the King. And therefore, nothing and no one can steal your joy.

"Joy is the flag which is flown from the castle of
the heart when the King is in residence there," said
Principal Rainy. So dear friend, fly His flag today!

Father, I take courage because I know that You are on my side and that You will stay by my side through it all. Amen.

Live through Every Season

There is a time for everything, and a season for every activity under the heavens. (Ecclesiastes 3:1)

Our dear Father designed His creation with so much incredibly intricate detail. The mere fact that He created different seasons just makes so much sense in light of the entire ecological system, the flow of nature, the cultivation of agricultural crops … and even in our own lives.

Just imagine what it would have been like if it was always winter, if we had to wear thick coats to shield us from the icy cold all year round. Or if we had to endure scorching heatwaves for all twelve months of the year. And even though the middle seasons are more balmy and bearable, it would also not have been pleasant to have falling autumn leaves or spring allergies all through the year.

Likewise, God gives us different seasons in our lives; times when joy blooms brightly in our hearts, times when we need more of His warm love, times when losses strip our hearts of all greenery and times when our lives enter a new pleasant phase of growth.

Live life to the full in every season of your life,
because who knows how long this one may last?

Thank You for all the variation in my life, please help me to live through each and every phase. Amen.

Celebrate Life

All the days of the oppressed are wretched, but the cheerful heart has a continual feast. (Proverbs 15:15)

How do you see life? Do you see the glass half full or half empty? Do you feel that people are negative towards you or do you take note of their genuine smiles? Do you think that life is just too hard or are you focused on the privilege of being alive?

If a person looks only at the holes, you would think that a screen door is useless. And yet it keeps the flies out. This is a philosophy put forward by an anonymous author.

When our Creator made us, He intended us to be happy people. He dreamt of how His children would live happy lives and love Him and other people unconditionally. Well now, a lot of things have changed in the meantime and daily we are faced with things that tend to make us negative and bitter. But, if we choose to stay positive in spite of it all, life will look and feel completely different. And then we will indeed be able to enjoy life even in the midst of all the imperfection.

Decide to celebrate life today! You will be surprised at how much of a feast it really is.

Create in me a heart that shouts for joy, Father. Amen.

Always Be Content

I have learned to be content whatever the circumstances.
(Philippians 4:11)

The grass is not greener on the other side of the fence! Now, how many times have we thought that happiness can be found in a different place or different circumstances. Just to finally get there … and still feel discontent. The fact of the matter is that deep-rooted inner joy is not dependent on places, people or circumstances. The attitude of your heart is the drive behind true happiness.

When you live your life closely connected to the Holy Spirit, like Paul did, a miracle takes place in your heart. It will enable you to have joy, just like he did, despite being poverty stricken or well-off and having very little or way too much. And then you can also say: "I can do all this through Him [Christ] who gives me strength" (Phil. 4:13).

So today, remember Lou Holtz's words, "Ability is what you're capable of doing. Motivation determines what you do. Attitude determines how well you do it."

Teach me how to have a heart like Paul's – one that is content. Amen.

Refuse to Let Your Joy Be Stolen

The weapons we fight with are not the weapons of the world. On the contrary, they have divine power to demolish strongholds.
(2 Corinthians 10:4)

The day you decided to give your life to the Lord, Satan started sharpening the weapons he uses to attack you. When you told God that it is your genuine desire to do only His will, your battle against evil commenced in all fierceness. Because the Evil One is determined to steal your peace and joy in life.

There is but one way to resist the attacks that Satan launches on your life and that is to hold on to your Father's hand with all your might. Never start even one day of your life without first praying and asking for the Lord's protection. Also make sure that your faith, your knowledge of God and willingness to do His will become greater day after day.

Therefore, stay on your knees day after day. Stay on God's side. That is what it means to be truly happy.

Strengthen me, Father God. Make me strong enough to remain faithful – and therefore also happy. Amen.

September

The Courage to Give

"The endless pursuit of wealth means giving away your own freedom. Golden chains are no less chains than chains of iron."

~ François Fénelon

When Jesus heard this, He said to him, "You still lack one thing. Sell everything you have and give to the poor, and you will have treasure in heaven. Then come, follow Me."

~ Luke 18:22

Live a Fulfilling Life

He reached down from on high and took hold of me; He drew me out of deep waters. (Psalm 18:16)

You may have considered skipping over September's readings when you saw the topic for this month. Maybe you are just not up to adding even more obligations to your already overwhelming to-do list. Or maybe you feel so empty inside that you just don't think you have anything left to give.

All women go through such low-tide times. The fact of the matter is that we can only give when we are full. Yes, only when we are full of energy, hope and love, are we able to give something of ourselves to others. And that is why it is so important for you to make time every day to nourish, rest and care for your body, soul and spirit.

Yes, you have to make time for that yourself. Other people are certainly not going to give you that all-important me-time.

Now, relax and allow the Spirit to fill you
with His caring and all-encompassing power.

Spirit of God, You know how empty my heart feels. Please give me Your strength and Your courage to face this day. Amen.

Call a Halt

You, LORD, keep my lamp burning; my God turns my darkness into light. With Your help I can advance against a troop; with my God I can scale a wall. (Psalm 18:28-29)

The fact that you're a woman means that you are usually busy offering someone else support. Naturally, you are responsible for managing the household, for looking after your family's physical and spiritual needs, you may even have a career as well as one hundred and one additional obligations.

You like your life … but sometimes it feels as if the last little drop of your energy has been squeezed out of you! That is when you feel fragile, vulnerable and discouraged about the never-ending routine and responsibilities in your life. I myself have also gone through times in my life when it felt like everything was too much for me to handle; times when I neglected myself, others and my relationship with God.

In those times, self-pity and the accompanying tears brought me some relief from the emotions of feeling overwhelmed, but it didn't solve the problem of my too-full schedule.

There is only one person that can call a halt when things get too much … you! Decide when and where you are going to do it today. Then go and do it. Come on, you owe it to yourself.

Dear Father, I am utterly exhausted. Show me how to take time and be still … next to You. Amen.

Manage Your Life

Fear of man will prove to be a snare, but whoever trusts in the LORD is kept safe. (Proverbs 29:25)

When you reach the point where you are in tatters and completely empty because you have given all of yourself, you have a huge responsibility towards yourself. You owe it to yourself to manage the tides in your life in such a way that you have the opportunity to rest and recover your strength during low tides as that will enable you take courage and carry on.

While He was here on earth, our dear Lord Jesus also went through times when things, people and responsibilities just got too much. And yet, He had the discipline to manage it all by:

- regularly making time to speak to the Father in isolation;
- turning His back on the crowds so that He and His disciples could find peace again; and
- striking a healthy balance between His work, friends and social duties.

Your Father really wants to see you living a happy and fulfilling life. So, allow the Holy Spirit to show you how to manage your life so that you can achieve just that.

O Spirit of God, help me to be a more balanced ... and happy person. Amen.

Live through All the Stages

Take delight in the LORD, and He will give you the desires of your heart. Commit your way to the LORD; trust in Him and He will do this ... (Psalm 37:4-5)

It is really easy to give of yourself to others when you feel good. In those times, you generously give out friendliness, assistance and support to others. And typically when you feel full enough to share some of yourself with others, you automatically feel more fulfilled.

But now what about those times when you feel so down, tired and empty that you have nothing to offer anyone? Maybe that is when you should afford yourself some cocoon-time; a time during which you isolate yourself so that you have the opportunity to rediscover your true self.

A time during which you drink deeply of God's Word and listen to His voice. And then ... then the time will come when you have to come out of your cocoon and spread your wings so that you can share some of the beauty in you with other people.

In which season do you currently find yourself:
Cocoon-time or butterfly-time? Think about it and then
live through and enjoy that phase for what it is.

Father, You understand me fully. Thank You for being there for me during all the stages of my life. Amen.

Give of Yourself

The LORD replied to them: "I am sending you grain, new wine and olive oil, enough to satisfy you fully." (Joel 2:19)

Isolating yourself from the world and affording yourself the opportunity to rediscover your true self is sometimes just what your heart needs. But then the time comes when we have to force ourselves to face the world again. When we spend too much time living in a cocoon … we are overcome by loneliness and self-pity. However, the wonderful thing is that when we open our eyes, ears and hearts to others – even in our times of difficulty – then our own problems often seem smaller and a lot less significant.

Yes, when we shift our focus to the pain and suffering of others and when we offer them support, we are also empowered to work through our own hardships bit by bit.

The lows will always become highs again and then you can ride the waves of joy. So when you are going through a tough time, try to reach out to others in distress – by doing this, you will receive inexplicable grace that will enable you to survive and overcome.

Give … even when it feels like you can't. You will
be surprised at how much you receive if you do.

Loving God, teach me to give of myself even in times of difficulty. Amen.

Influence Your Friends

Since we live by the Spirit, let us keep in step with the Spirit.
(Galatians 5:25)

"Obesity is contagious" was the heading on the front page of the newspaper a while back, and the accompanying article alleged that people are a lot more likely to become obese if their friends are overweight. Apparently, we much more readily acquire the habits of the people who we like.

That is why we feel a lot less guilty when we do wrong things with others and also why we feel good when we share good things with friends.

What do your friends learn from you? What are the characteristics that you display? Are there things that you do that others seem to want to emulate? If there is one way to enrich the lives of your friends … it is to set a Christlike example. Ask yourself the following question today, "Do I live in such a way that others can see Jesus in me? And is the example I am setting with my life such that other people will want to emulate it?"

Pray that the Holy Spirit will control your life so that you will influence others to also live in and through Him.

Spirit of God, sanctify me and help me to live in a way that will make other people want to be like You. Amen.

Make Others Rich

But the fruit of the Spirit is love, joy, peace, forbearance, kindness, goodness, faithfulness, gentleness and self-control.
(Galatians 5:22-23)

You don't have to be rolling in the money in order to make others rich. You only need to belong to Christ. Because, according to Galatians, then our lives will be like trees that bear much fruit that others can pick and enjoy.

Because Christ followers have their hearts' root systems securely anchored, being fed by the grace of the Spirit and watered with the living waters of the Word, their lives offer an abundance of good fruit to all those around them.

The Spirit compels these people to share the beauty of their own spirit with others. So, make sure that your heart is filled today – and every day – with the power contained in the Scriptures and the goodness of the Holy Spirit. Because then spontaneously sharing the riches of Christ's gracious love will feel like the most natural thing on earth.

Today, be generous with your love. Because
the more you give, the more you will receive.

Fill my heart to the brim with Your goodness, Lord, so that I can offer the fruit of the Spirit to others in abundance. Amen.

Say, "This Is Enough!"

Whoever loves money never has enough; whoever loves wealth is never satisfied with their income. (Ecclesiastes 5:10)

Money cannot buy happiness, but a lot of people want to put this to the test. When will you have enough money? If you get a salary increase, if you inherit a few hundred thousand dollars? Yes, the majority of people want more; more wealth, more possessions … more of everything. And then?

As soon as we have more, we simply adjust our standard of living and in a few months' time we wish for more again. All of a sudden we even struggle to stick to our bigger budget! Yes, enough just never seems to be enough!

Maybe we need to start thinking about money differently. Maybe we should ask ourselves the following questions: "What can I do with what I have? How can I be the best steward of what I have been given?"

True wealth for your soul lies in knowing
when to say, "I already have enough."

Show me how to find a balance, Father. Amen.

Give Away

Good will come to those who are generous and lend freely, who conduct their affairs with justice. (Psalm 112:5)

What a paradox: we have to give in order to receive! This makes no sense to the worldly-trained mind, after all, from a very young age we are taught that you must take what you can get. That's what life is all about, isn't it? Having more and being more powerful, richer and better than other people.

So in some or other way, we all suffer from this obtain-more-even-though-we-have-enough syndrome. The irony, however, is that often-times the more we have, the poorer we feel.

There is no way that we can set wealth against religion. There are wonderful children of God that are well-to-do and that make a huge difference in other people's lives. But we must never think that the pursuit of wealth is a recipe for a happy soul.

The Word makes it very clear: our souls are only as rich as we are generous in giving things away.

Jesus was penniless and yet He left us a priceless inheritance – eternal life.

How full is the treasure chamber of your soul?

Master, teach me to give: my talents, my gifts, my material possessions, my time ... to give myself to others. Amen.

SEPTEMBER 10

Be Poor

Believers in humble circumstances ought to take pride in their high position. (James 1:9)

What do you think the walls and streets in heaven are made of? Gold, marble, valuable gemstones? Maybe. One thing is for certain, though; every eternal brick was laid with the riches of our heavenly Father's grace. And that means that heaven is a dwelling place paved with God's great love from corner to corner. So, why don't we start living out some of the heavenly riches here on earth so long?

- We can experience heavenly wealth when we live our lives in total dependence on Him. It will remind us that we are nothing in and of ourselves.
- We feel rich when we are in His presence. After all, the very best place to be is at the feet of our Master.
- We can make His love our own and then express it. That is how we can live out His image.

Today, store up treasures for yourself where
moths and rust cannot destroy them.

Thank You for letting me experience heavenly wealth now already, Giver of Grace. Amen.

The Gift of Really Giving

She went away and did as Elijah had told her. So there was food every day for Elijah and for the woman and her family. For the jar of flour was not used up and the jug of oil did not run dry, in keeping with the word of the LORD spoken by Elijah. (1 Kings 17:15-16)

When does one really give? When we give because we have more than enough for ourselves or when we give what we desperately need ourselves – when giving means we have to do without.

In 1 Kings 17, we see that Elijah asked the poor widow to use her last little bit of olive oil and flour to make him a small loaf of bread. She complied with his request even though she actually only had enough oil and flour left to bake some bread for her son and herself. They thought that they would eat it and then die of starvation. But when we read on, we see that a miracle took place in her very own kitchen. The flour and oil just never ran out!

To really give asks something of you. It asks that part of your income that you wanted to spend on yourself, it asks some of your precious time and it asks a big part of your selfish heart.

Ask yourself this question: How much of myself do I really give?

Forgive my self-indulgence and selfishness and teach me how to live with open hands and an open heart, please Lord. Amen.

Master the Art of Giving

"Truly I tell you," He said, "this poor widow has put in more than all the others." (Luke 21:3)

Most of us like to comfort ourselves with the idea that at least we contribute to the church or charity organizations on a regular basis. But that is all it is: a comfort. Very few of us will be willing to put our last few coins in the collection plate or to empty out our purse to help someone else in need. After all, that is our hard-earned money!

Well now, that means that we would also have felt embarrassed about our supposed generosity that day in the temple when the poor widow came along and put all she had to live on in the temple treasury. We tend to reason that giving away all you have is just asking too much.

So, Jesus' response is also relevant for us today: that woman is a thousand times richer than all those people (and you) who contribute out of wealth and abundance.

Giving like that poor widow certainly is not easy. And yet, Jesus says that people who give like that are the ones that are really rich. May it encourage us to really give.

Teach me to give, gracious Father. Amen.

Open Your Heart

"You will always have the poor among you, but you will not always have Me." (John 12:8)

Six days before Passover, Jesus paid a visit to His friends and Mary walked into the room holding a flask of pure nard. To all the guests' surprise, she opened the container and poured all the very expensive perfume on her Master's feet after which she softly wiped away the excess oil with her hair.

While she performed this act of love, Judas piped up in the background, "Why are you wasting money by doing that?" Sly fox that he was, Judas said this because he was thinking only of enriching himself and because he didn't think that his Master deserved the special treatment. After all, at more than one occasion in the past he had helped himself to the money in Jesus' money bag … later on, he even sold out his Master for 30 silver coins!

It is very easy to feel antipathy towards Judas … but we have to be honest with ourselves. How often do we spend His time and His money on what we want?

Let's pray and ask the Father to transform our own Judas hearts to Mary hearts so that we can give from our hearts.

Forgive me for being so selfish, Lord, and open my heart to You. Amen.

Weigh Your Words

Set a guard over my mouth, Lord; keep watch over the door of my lips. (Psalm 141:3)

There are a lot of things in life that we can just give out in innumerable quantities, like love and heartfelt compassion, forgiveness, acceptance, kindness and goodness. However, there is one thing that we must weigh before we give it to others … we must weigh our words.

Especially seeing as our words tend to be impure, inconsiderate, inappropriate and rude. Words can hurt other people, damage their self-esteem and steal their sense of worth. Johann Wolfgang von Goethe confirms this by saying that a word wounds a lot easier than it heals.

To always say the right thing is a gift of the Holy Spirit. It is something that we will only manage to get right if our hearts and thoughts are tuned into God. Then we will be able to make beautiful sounds that harmonize with the symphony of love. If, however, we are not tuned into God, we will utter nothing but terribly false notes.

Day after day, pray and ask your Father to put a
guard at the door of your lips so that His Spirit will
only let the words pass that are pure and right.

Spirit of God, let the words that come out of my mouth testify that my heart and thoughts are pure. Amen.

Live a Purified Life

My brothers and sisters, can a fig tree bear olives, or a grapevine bear figs? Neither can a salt spring produce fresh water. (James 3:12)

Humankind is seriously in need of pure drinking water. The challenge to supply people with clean water is one that everyone faces, from the first to the third world countries.

This unresolved issue along with all the others is, however, not all we have to contend with as strife, revolts, revolutions, wars and violence are all on the rise as well. The reason for this is that the wellspring of human purity – namely, our hearts – has become muddy!

You and I may not be able to change the world, but we can make a difference in the lives of the people around us. That is why we have to ensure that our hearts are pure, because then the Spirit will have the opportunity to work in and through us. We will see how our lives and the lives of others are enriched when all the fruit of the Spirit are visible, audible and tangible in our lives.

Leo Tolstoy said, "Everyone thinks of changing
the world, but no one thinks of changing
himself." Let's prove him wrong today!

Holy Spirit, make my heart pure and brand new today. Amen.

Live with Abandon

Vindicate me, LORD, for I have led a blameless life; I have trusted in the LORD and have not faltered. (Psalm 26:1)

David was a man who had the courage to really live. He was brave enough to confront a giant, but he also allowed himself to be vulnerable enough to pour out his heart to God.

He was serious about God and His Word and he was human enough to repent after having committed adultery. He accepted that all authority lies with God, but he also shouldered his responsibilities faithfully. He was able to cry just as loudly as he sang God's praises and he would both shout for joy and be left speechless in awe of his Lord … because he knew who he was worshipping.

Are you truly alive? Or are you hiding behind a mask of pretense and living a lie? Do you know what, dear heart, we were created to live our lives to the full. We were also created to worship God with our entire being and all our emotions.

> God is challenging you today: live your life
> to the full with Me. So, go and do just that!

Father, help me to experience all of life's facets today along with Your greatness. Amen.

Spread Joy

The fruit of the Spirit is … joy. (Galatians 5:22)

I am amazed by people who are really suffering … and yet always smiling. Or those who, despite all the burdens that they have had to bear, still keep their heads up in humble self-confidence. And then there are those that drive around in their fancy cars … while looking terribly unhappy and frustrated.

Clearly, true happiness has nothing to do with your material possessions or comforts. It has to do with something much deeper.

Happy people spontaneously add to other people's lives. They multiply the joys of life. In contrast to that, disgruntled people are the ones that take something out of your life. So, ask yourself this, "Are you adding to other people's lives by living out the joy of the Holy Spirit or are you draining others with your negativity and unfriendliness?"

Pray that you will have the ability to,
despite your circumstances, share the deep-
rooted joy of being a child of God with others.

Put Your kind of joy in my heart today, Spirit of God. Amen.

Share God's Peace with Others

The fruit of the Spirit is … peace. (Galatians 5:22)

World peace is what she wants to achieve, said every aspiring beauty queen in her bid to become the next Miss World. Global conferences all over the world also debate the hot topic of world peace. "How can we establish peace in our country?" we sigh when we read of another murder in the newspaper and we say, "Peace be with you!" when we wish each other well.

We are all striving to live a peaceful life: a life lived in peace with God, other people and ourselves. And yet we never seem to reach that point of real peacefulness … and that is because we are struggling to truly live Spirit-filled lives.

On our own, we may not be able to achieve world peace, but with the help of the Holy Spirit we can certainly change our hearts, which will in turn change the lives of others for the better.

> Day after day, ask the Spirit to remove all unpeace
> from your heart and to fill it with His kind of peace:
> a peace that understands, forgives and reconciles.

Lord, it is not always easy to live in peace with others and myself. Please come to my aid in my weakness. Amen.

Let Peace Start with You

"Peace I leave with you; my peace I give to you. Not as the world gives do I give to you. Let not your hearts be troubled, neither let them be afraid." (John 14:27)

Peace starts with sanctification, or purification. And because we are human, we have more than enough impurities in and around us.

There is sin that leaves us restless, unforgiveness that encumbers us, anxiety as well as a host of other things that try to steal our divine peace. So, before we try to share this peace with others, we need to allow the Holy Spirit to purify every corner of our hearts. Only then will we be able to live out God's peace towards others in our thoughts, words and deeds.

It is no easy feat to maintain true peace in your hearts and share it with others. In and of ourselves, we are much too hopeless and weak to accomplish it. But thank the Lord! Because we have the Spirit of peace that helps us in our weakness.

Keep praying that God will fill you with His peace
that surpasses all understanding. Then He will have
the opportunity to let world peace start with you!

God of peace, sanctify me and make me a person of peace. Amen.

Turn Away from Unpeace

Speak and act as those who are going to be judged by the law that gives freedom, because judgment without mercy will be shown to anyone who has not been merciful. Mercy triumphs over judgment. (James 2:12-13)

Satan has a thousand and one ways to lure us away from God ... so that he can put unpeace in our hearts! Spirit-filled children of God know this all too well. And that is why they purposely try to resist Satan's influence every day.

Furthermore, children of peace turn and run away from sin without delay. They know that they simply cannot insist on receiving God's kindness and peace if they deliberately go against His will and commit sin. There is absolutely no way that we can live in peace with ourselves and the world around us if we allow sin to have a hold on our lives.

Are you continually listening to the whispers of
the Holy Spirit in your heart? Do you obey Him?
Do you turn your back on sin or do you cherish it?

Lord, today I realize that I will only have peace in my heart and peace to share with others if I obey You. Amen.

SEPTEMBER 21

Be Patient

The fruit of the Spirit is ... patience. (Galatians 5:22)

Humankind has become so impatient and intolerant towards one another. Just think of how easily we become irritated when other people don't do what we want them to or when we misunderstand each other. And then the words we say to each other are so vicious and derogatory.

There is one thing that will really make a difference to the lives of the people around you, and that is you being more tolerant of them today. In this way, you will automatically share some of God's acceptance-love with them – accept them for who they are, offer them compassion and heartfelt care.

God has more than enough reason to be irritated with us. We certainly are not angels that do as He says and behave as He expects of us. And yet … He tolerates us day after day with great grace, patience and love.

> God gives us His gracious love unconditionally
> and in abundance. So, let's share some of
> this love with other people today.

Dear Holy Spirit, give me the courage to be tolerant of everyone today. Amen.

Give Selfless Love

Those who give to the poor will lack nothing, but those who close their eyes to them receive many curses. (Proverbs 28:27)

Most of us are quite willing to give if we know that we will get something in return. Most of the time, we first think how is this going to benefit us …

In Luke 14:12-14, Jesus teaches us that the people who cannot repay us in any way are precisely the ones that we are supposed to spoil with our goodness. He says that when we are good to the poor, the crippled, the lame, the blind and those that are suffering, we will be truly happy and blessed. He also adds that "you will be repaid at the resurrection of the righteous" (Luke 14:14).

The Word teaches us that giving should not be a trade, but that we should just give ourselves unconditionally and without expecting something in return. So, when the Spirit prompts you to do something for someone or to give something to someone, do it without reserve, because that is how we can truly live out some of God's love.

Ask the Spirit to show you where, how and to whom
you need to go and give some of your selfless love.

Heavenly Father, please teach me the language of unselfish love. Amen.

Give without Reserve

You will be enriched in every way so that you can be generous on every occasion, and through us your generosity will result in thanksgiving to God. (2 Corinthians 9:11)

You might have seen the movie *Pay it Forward* and it probably made you think twice, didn't it? It is the story of a young boy who gave without expecting anything in return and how this behavior of his totally revolutionized his community.

After the example he set, people were suddenly all very eager to find out how and where they could help others or what they could give away … without expecting anything in return. Over time, this pattern became a habit. And the givers' unconditional goodwill towards others was rewarded with rich blessings time after time.

When you give without reserve, it is never in vain. The Word tells us that God will wrap the cheerful and generous giver in His goodness.

Why don't you start a revolution of giving in your own social circle? Yes, wholeheartedly give something of yourself to the people around you today. In this way, you will let generosity snowball.

Lord Jesus, help me to give myself to others, like You did, without a list of terms and conditions. Amen.

Share Your Heart

And God is able to bless you abundantly, so that in all things at all times, having all that you need, you will abound in every good work. (2 Corinthians 9:8)

If you're affluent, giving away a few dollars hardly makes a difference to your bank balance. If you are someone whose purse is open to others, so to speak, you are truly blessed as you are in service of the greater Kingdom.

Jesus, however, came and taught that giving is about much more than just your purse being open. The heavenly way of giving means that you make yourself available to others. For instance, someone might be in need of your patient ear, your hands, feet, wisdom or advice. People are quite often also in need of your precious time.

And then there are times when people need … your heart. The heart that listens with understanding and compassion, that offers comfort and that really cares.

People need each other's hearts-of-love. Are you willing to share yours with someone else today?

Lord, please teach me the heart's language of love. Amen.

Leave It up to Him

"I make known the end from the beginning, from ancient times, what is still to come." (Isaiah 46:10)

Most of us can strongly associate with Rick Warren's statement about life being a series of problems that need to be solved. It really does feel like the next problem is always waiting just around the corner – as soon as we have solved one problem, the next is upon us. Unfortunately, that is just the way things are: worries, challenges and discomforts are all a part of life.

Paul had the ability to face this fact of life and deal with it, because he saw his great God in every earthly problem. And that is why he could say that he didn't allow life to get the better of him, to make him feel depressed or disheartened or to keep him down.

Maybe you and I should pray that we will surrender our hearts in every and all circumstances, that we will have hearts full of courage to face the day because we placed every aspect of our lives in the hands of the living God.

Leave every part of your life up to the
Father. He will deal with it for you.

Thank You for making everything possible! Amen.

Relinquish Your "Independence"

You whom I have upheld since your birth, and have carried since you were born. (Isaiah 46:3)

In a world where our independence and self-reliance are the pre-requisites for human dignity, it is not easy to practice the exact opposite. And that is why we find it so hard to be fully dependent on God.

Like rebellious teenagers, we choose to try and provide for ourselves while God actually wants to take care of us, just like a loving Father cares for His children. How silly of us! Our dear Father is able to and really wants to carry us in His arms of grace, look after us and guide us day after day.

Of course, God won't do what we are supposed to do for us, but when we do our part, then we can relax and leave the rest in His hands.

Allow the words in Isaiah 46:4 to inspire you to surrender to Him fully, "Even to your old age and grey hairs, I am He, I am He who will sustain you. I have made you and I will carry you; I will sustain you and I will rescue you."

Lord, please sustain me today … and always! Amen.

Bring Everyone before Him

A gentle answer turns away wrath, but a harsh word stirs up anger.
(Proverbs 15:1)

Relationships between people are very much like a field of landmines. Just when you think everything in your relationships is going well … a bomb goes off. Someone misunderstands you, you have to make unwelcome decisions, others judge you or irritation causes conflict and tension between people.

And that is why it is so very important that we give ourselves, our family members, our colleagues at work and everyone that may come our way to the Father every day. He is the only One who can disarm every landmine in every situation, who can create compassion in human hearts and who can enable people to treat each other with love and understanding.

So today, give your own heart and every single person in your life to your Father. Ask Him to make your hearts sensitive towards each other and to help you to have divine understanding, acceptance and love in your relationship with one another.

May all your relationships be good, blessed and full of joy.

Lord of my life, let Your Spirit live among us today, please. Amen.

SEPTEMBER 28

Leave It to Him

Humble yourselves, therefore, under God's mighty hand, that He may lift you up in due time. Cast all your anxiety on Him because He cares for you. (1 Peter 5:6-7)

Have you also had sleepless nights because of questions like: Why did that have to happen? Why did he or she act like that? How could things possibly go so wrong? What am I supposed to do now? … Lord, what is Your will?

Despite our best intentions to live a life of love and peace, we are still sometimes confronted with situations where we just don't know which way to turn. These are the situations that leave us feeling stunned and speechless, silently wondering, "What is the reason for this and what am I supposed to do now?"

These are the times when we just need to completely surrender and place everything and everyone in God's hands. Because our almighty Father already knows all the answers to all the whys and the hows and the what-must-I-do-nows?

Stop grappling with unanswered questions and remember: your Father knows. Give everything that you are struggling with to Him and then wait expectantly to see how He will miraculously sort things out for you.

Faithful Father, please take control over every aspect of my life. Amen.

Give It to Him

On that day they will say to Jerusalem, "Do not fear, Zion; do not let your hands hang limp. The LORD your God is with you, the Mighty Warrior who saves. He will take great delight in you; in His love He will no longer rebuke you, but will rejoice over you with singing."
(Zephaniah 3:16-17)

We all know the Serenity Prayer that goes, "God grant me the serenity to accept the things I cannot change; courage to change the things I can; and wisdom to know the difference."

And yet, we don't always manage to leave the things that we cannot change or control in the Father's hands. Time and again, we go to Him and take the matter back into our own hands and then we worry ourselves sick about it again (or still!)

So, in every situation, ask yourself the following question: Which part of this is my responsibility? And then you do that. Give the rest to Him without holding anything back and then leave it in His hands. He knows. And He is able. And He will deal with it for you.

May you be full of courage every step of the way today.

Father, how great are You! Help me to trust You unconditionally. Amen.

Find Rest in Him

*[May our Lord Jesus Christ Himself and God our Father] encourage
your hearts and strengthen you in every good deed and word.
(2 Thessalonians 2:17)*

Have you ever woken up in a panic; being gripped by fear as you
wrestle with all your problems in an attempt at finding solutions; while
wondering how you are going to survive and dreading the future? Or
maybe you have had things happen to you that were so bad that you
just wanted to pull the blanket over your head and forget about it all.

The author of Lamentations most probably also felt like that
when he wrote the five sad songs about the sorry state and terrible
circumstances in which the believers of those times found themselves.

He says, "I remember my affliction and my wandering, the bitterness
and the gall. I well remember them, and my soul is downcast within
me." But then he adds, "Yet this I call to mind and therefore I have
hope: because of the LORD's great love we are not consumed, for His
compassions never fail" (Lam. 3:19-22).

May God also grant you hope and rest for your soul today.

Thank You, Savior, that I can find peace with You. Amen.

October

The Courage to Be Different

*"Men are like trees: each one must put forth
the leaf that is created in him."*

~ Henry Ward Beecher

*And we all, who with unveiled faces contemplate the Lord's glory,
are being transformed into His image with ever-increasing glory,
which comes from the Lord, who is the Spirit.*

~ 2 Corinthians 3:18

Be Different

I am Your servant; give me discernment that I may understand Your statutes. (Psalm 119:125)

You might be wondering why there is any need for anything to be different. Your life is more or less as it should be, there are not too many things that are off track and you feel fairly safe and comfortable in your own skin. You have also learnt to live with the weak links in your life-chain and you have made peace with who you are as a person.

The answer lies in these words: the difference between a groove and a grave is only a matter of depth.

Our dear Father doesn't want us to chastise ourselves for who we are or who we are not, or for what we do or don't do. His gracious love accepts us just the way we are. But if we really want to live a fulfilling spiritual life, grow in our relationship with Him and others and receive even more heavenly riches, then we simply can't stay where we are.

So today, accept the challenge to develop your heart and soul this month. There are so many more riches in life that are yet to be discovered.

Thank You, Master of my life, that I can grow through You. Amen.

Necessary Change

For this is what the LORD Almighty says: "After the Glorious One has sent me against the nations that have plundered you – for whoever touches you touches the apple of His eye …" (Zachariah 2:8)

There is a German proverb that goes like this: to change and to improve are two different things. Change for the sake of change makes no sense; but when change results in improvement, growth and leads to the best outcome, then the discomfort that comes along with it is always worth it. Just like in the old days when God's people kept wandering off. He knew that His children were headed for a fall and that is why He repeatedly called them back to Him in various different ways.

Even today, our faithful God still has a way of warning us and calling us back to obedience to Him when we wander off. So, be grateful when the Spirit makes you feel unsettled about the things in your life that are not right. It can mean only one thing: your Father deems you valuable enough to be involved in your life by calling your attention to the things that need changing.

God brings us out of the dark – not to judge
us, but to say, "Return to Me, apple of My eye.
Things are so much better here with Me."

Let my entire being come close to You, Father. Amen.

Comfort Zones

For God is working in you, giving you the desire and the power to do what pleases Him. (Philippians 2:13)

It is always easier to just stay in your comfort zone. After all, that is where we feel safe and secure. So why change anything if everything more or less works?

The fact of the matter is that the Spirit of God will not make you feel unsettled about areas in your life for no reason. He only draws our attention to those aspects of our lives that He wants us to change, so that our lives can be different. He might be showing you how to change your way of living from being more-or-less-right to heavenly and fulfilled.

The Spirit always has a reason for everything He does and He also has a divine responsibility when working in the hearts of God's children. So, you can rest assured that it is in your best interest if He draws your attention to something that you need to do differently by making your heart feel unsettled about it. Remember, God doesn't only change things, He improves them! Maybe not in the way that we expect Him to, but nonetheless, in a way that will be to your benefit.

Know this: your Father is on your side.
Even when He calls you out of your comfort zone.

Lord, show me what You want me to change about my life. And help me to hear You. Amen.

Live Out Love

Don't let anyone look down on you because you are young, but set an example for the believers in speech, in conduct, in love, in faith and in purity. (1 Timothy 4:12)

Someone once said that it doesn't matter what the question is, the answer is always … love. Because love changes people's hearts, their lives, their relationships and their happiness. The opposite of love – things like anger, unforgiveness, grudges and hate – has the exact opposite effect. It turns us into people whose lives are filled with discord, discontent and dissatisfaction.

Think about it: how many things in your life will change if you deal with it in love? Are there broken or difficult relationships in your life that can be mended with love? How will your perspective on situations change if your approach is one of love? When you muster the courage to approach every aspect of your life with a heart filled with love, you will find that everything will suddenly look different.

Pray every morning for the Holy Spirit to bless you abundantly with the kind of love that will show the world that you are different: that you are a child of God.

Father, I am here to make a difference. Show me how. Amen.

Have Respect for God

And she made a vow, saying, "LORD Almighty, if You will only look on Your servant ..." (1 Samuel 1:11)

I'm sure you have also lost hope from time to time, particularly when you prayed about something for a very long time and it felt like God wasn't answering your prayer. Just like Hannah so many years ago. She badly wanted a son, but remained childless year after year. For years she begged the Lord: "Please give me a son" and month after month, His answer was, "Not now, My child. Not now."

When we sit with unanswered prayers, questions and requests, it is easy to start doubting God's love for us. We may even become impatient or angry with our Father. It is in times like these that we want to call out: "But Lord, I don't understand!" The fact of the matter is this: God is God. So, the answer to every prayer and every single breakthrough depend solely on His will and power. All we have to do is to keep trusting Him unconditionally – even in the times that we don't understand – and to know that He will give us the perfect answer at the right time.

Remain God's humble and faithful servant
in all circumstances. He does hear you!

I honor You with all my heart, Lord ... even though I don't understand. Amen.

Honor Him

Then Hannah prayed and said, "My heart rejoices in the LORD; in the LORD my horn is lifted high. My mouth boasts over my enemies, for I delight in Your deliverance." (1 Samuel 2:1)

Can you imagine how happy the childless Hannah must have been when she gave birth to her son, Samuel – who she obtained through prayer. Yes, we all know that feeling of relief mixed with joy when things in our lives work out well, when we get a breakthrough or when we are surprised by good news. And then … it is all too easy to forget all about God and to take the credit for ourselves.

Everything that we are, that we receive and that we achieve is pure grace from the hand of our loving Father. So, we must honor Him in all circumstances. Especially when He answers our prayers, blesses us and showers us with His goodness and thus brings joy into our lives.

Honor your Father for everything in your life:
the nice as well as the not-so-nice things. By doing
that, you will halve the bad and double the good.

Thank You, Lord, for changing my sorrow into joy time after time. Amen.

Keep Your Promises

[Hannah] said to him, "Pardon me, my lord. As surely as you live, I am the woman who stood here beside you praying to the Lord. I prayed for this child, and the Lord has granted me what I asked of Him." (1 Samuel 1:26-27)

It must have been very hard for Hannah to keep her promise to the Lord. She had wanted a son for so many years and now she had to give him back to God – just as she had promised to do – so he could go and work in the temple. It meant that she would only get to see him once a year. Ouch!

And yet Hannah remains faithful and she tells Eli: "So now I give him (Samuel) to the Lord. For his whole life he will be given over to the Lord" (1 Sam. 1:28).

When we make a promise to the Lord it is a very serious matter. Because then our Father expects us to be faithful and to keep our word – no matter how hard it may be.

May you and I have the courage to remain faithful
to our conscience and keep our promises.

Guide of my life, help me to never ignore Your voice for the sake of my own comfort. Amen.

Listen Very Carefully

The boy Samuel ministered before the LORD under Eli. In those days the word of the LORD was rare; there were not many visions.
(1 Samuel 3:1)

There is a French proverb saying that God visits us, but most of the time we are not at home. Yes, God does not shout His instructions at us and He never forces His will on people. He whispers when our hearts are ready to listen to Him. Just like when He called to the sleeping Samuel and revealed His will to the boy.

Do you have enough quiet time so that you can hear His voice speaking in your heart? Or do you allow the world and its noise to keep you too busy? Listening to God is a choice: you can choose to immediately hush the soft whisper of your conscience or you can listen expectantly to hear what He has to say. You will find that God works in divine and all-powerful ways in the lives of attentive children.

What do you do when God speaks to you?
Do you ignore Him or do you say what Samuel
said, "Speak, for Your servant is listening."

Comforter, please speak to me. I really do want to listen! Amen.

Listen to His Voice

Pray continually ... (1 Thessalonians 5:17)

It is not always easy to really listen. After all, we're living in a fast-paced era where things must get done quickly. We simply don't have the time to sit still and listen. And as a result, many of us rush from point A to point B every single day without getting any fulfillment from our existence.

And because we don't have the time to find out what God's will is for our lives, we miss our calling completely and so we are left feeling discontented and unhappy! Like Alice in Wonderland, we are headed to who knows where!

Don't you want to make some time to listen to what God has to say to you? Only He can tell you what your purpose is and what you need to do to fulfill it.

Make some quiet time today. Then allow the
Holy Spirit to speak to you. Then listen.
Listen again. And hear Him answering you!

Dear Father, teach me Your ways and Your will for my life. Teach me the right way to live! Amen.

Know What You Want

The human spirit is the lamp of the LORD that sheds light on one's inmost being. (Proverbs 20:27)

You can't hit the target if you don't know what you're aiming for. You first need to dream about and desire something, before you can take action to obtain it.

So, the question is: What are you striving for? What do you want to achieve? What do you want to be remembered for? Our dreams will all differ according to our unique personalities and the unique dream that God has for each of our lives.

When what God has planned for you, what you're striving for and what you're doing all line up, you will be happy. And your life will be meaningful, because you will be fulfilling your purpose.

If you know what your calling is and if you are already walking in it, then you are a very blessed person. If, however, you are still wondering what your purpose is and if it feels like your life has no meaning, then you can get the answer to your questions in only one place: on your knees.

Great God, why am I alive? Help me discover my purpose. Amen.

Change Your Thinking

Carefully guard your thoughts because they are the source of true life.
(Proverbs 4:23)

Have you ever considered the fact that you could be sabotaging yourself? That you have always stood in the way of being able to live a fulfilling life because you either don't believe in yourself or you don't have the courage to think differently? It is our thinking that enables us to do anything. You can either think that you are a failure and a perpetually unhappy person; or you can think that you are a successful person who finds joy in living a fulfilling life. You'll be spot on either way.

Now, it doesn't matter what your thought patterns were like in the past, because the Spirit of God can make them brand new. The One that knows you also knows what you are capable of and where your Creator wants to take you. So, He is also the One who can help you to think differently – to have new and improved thinking.

Pray for the renewal of your mind every morning so that your thinking will please God and so that you can celebrate life knowing and believing that you can win life's race through Him.

Make my thinking brand new today. So that I can live according to Your will for my life. Amen.

Find Your GPS

"I make known the end from the beginning, from ancient times, what is still to come." (Isaiah 46:10)

To think that we are responsible for our own lives and that our thought patterns determine the direction of our lives is quite a scary thought.

To be honest, it immediately makes you feel guilty about the way things have gone in your life and about the boring existence that you've brought on yourself. The fact is, however, that God gave each of us a built-in navigation system – a GPS – when He created us. Our GPS will guide us in the right direction. The problem is that most of us have never taken the time to listen to our heart's GPS or that we are not sensitive enough to hear its voice.

The Holy Spirit was given to us to guide each and every one of us in a miraculous way so that we can find and fulfill our calling here on earth.

Listen to the voice of the Holy Spirit in you more frequently.
You will be surprised at how doing just that will change your life.

Creator of the universe, direct my thoughts to what You have planned for my life. Amen.

Find Your Dream

Now the One who has fashioned us for this very purpose is God, who has given us the Spirit as a deposit, guaranteeing what is to come. (2 Corinthians 5:5)

No one else can tell you what your dream should be. You need to find it for yourself! Because your passion in life depends on your deepest desires, talents, gifts and abilities.

The sum total of all these things is the true you. When your mind, will and emotions are all in line with the dream that God placed inside you, then things will start to happen in your life. You will find yourself doing things you never thought yourself capable of doing, you will perform in ways that are beyond even your wildest dreams and then you will be happy with your life.

Very few people's dreams line up with what God has planned for them. And that is why more than two thirds of people are unhappy in their jobs and why they just want to get their daily stint over and done with as soon as possible.

Be sure to make time to really think and pray about your life, what you are and what God wants you to be. Because you will only find true happiness if you live out your divine dream.

Father God, I want to know Your dream for my life so that I can live it out. Amen.

Make Your Life Easier

Yet I am always with You; You hold me by my right hand. You guide me with Your counsel, and afterward You will take me into glory. (Psalm 73:23-24)

Over the last few days, you may have felt like you are just not up to facing even more challenges, making changes or discovering new dreams. Maybe you decided to just keep swimming in your familiar and ordinary life-stream without making too many waves.

Well now, if you are fulfilling your life's purpose, then you are already living a happy and positive life. But if you are feeling unhappy and unfulfilled with your life, then it means that you are swimming upstream and that you are not doing what you were created to do.

However, when your life is in line with God's will for you then you are swimming with the stream. You will be doing what you're good at, you will enjoy what you're doing and you will easily and comfortably live out your passion and calling.

Stop swimming upstream. Allow the Holy Spirit to show you what the natural flow of your life is and then follow it. Doing that will make your life a lot easier.

Help me to live my life in line with what You want for me, Counselor of my life. Amen.

Make Your Dream Work

Many are the plans in a person's heart, but it is the Lord's purpose that prevails. (Proverbs 19:21)

When you have discovered what your dream – your unique purpose in life – is, your whole life will change.

You will no longer get depressed on Sunday evenings because Monday morning is around the corner. You will also no longer feel like you need to complete your tasks as fast as possible just so that you can "get away from there". No, when you have discovered the secret of your passion and when you live it out, you will enjoy your vocation, you will identify and make use of opportunities and you will live a fulfilling life.

The wonder of it all is that when you live out your passion, you will not be the only one that derives benefit from it. It will be to the advantage of dozens of people – maybe even thousands of people.

You will not only be radiating enthusiasm and positive energy, but you will also have the ability to motivate others and have a positive impact on their lives. And because you live out your natural talents and interests, you will make a massive difference to the world through the power of the Holy Spirit that indwells you.

Is your dream working for you?
Is it working for God? And other people?

May my life serve both You and other people, Master. Amen.

Live Life to the Full

Sustain me, my God, according to Your promise, and I will live; do not let my hopes be dashed. (Psalm 119:116)

No dream that is worth it can be achieved without effort. No goal is reached without unexpected setbacks, temporary failures and even opposition. The secret, however, is to keep your eyes on the prize – no matter what – and to keep on trying. It is no different in our spiritual lives as it certainly is not smooth sailing all the way.

Paul openly attested to this fact of life when he said that he knows that he has not yet arrived at his goal, but that it will not deter him from pressing on. Just like a dedicated athlete preparing for the Olympic Games, he exerts himself to reach the finish line of faith. Yes, we cannot reach our final faith destination here on earth, but we continually have to make an effort to become stronger and better every day. So, hold on dear heart, hold on!

Live your life to the full today, being inspired
by C. S. Lewis's words: "There are better
things ahead than any we leave behind."

Thank You for being prepared to coach me, Your non-perfect athlete, every day. Amen.

Make Your Load Lighter

Give your burdens to the LORD, and He will take care of you. He will not permit the godly to slip and fall. (Psalm 55:22)

There is a very good reason for why athletes compete in races wearing the lightest possible clothing.

After all, we know that every little bit of extra weight is only to your own detriment and will keep you from doing your best. But now that makes me wonder why we tend to take so much baggage along on our faith-race. Yes, quite often we drag along all our past regrets, all our I-can'ts, all our insecurities and all our problems. And then we wonder why we're not making much progress!

One of the heroes of our faith is Paul who initially persecuted Christians and who had a thorn in his flesh that really bothered him, but he knew that to reach his goal he had to put all those things behind him for good. And that is why he was such an awe-inspiring Christian athlete for the faith.

Don't you want to take all your unnecessary baggage to the Cross today and leave it there so that you can strive for your faith-dream being more free and relieved?

Savior, today I leave my baggage permanently at the foot of the Cross. Amen.

Care for Your Body

Do you not know that your bodies are temples of the Holy Spirit, who is in you, whom you have received from God? You are not your own; you were bought at a price. Therefore honor God with your bodies.
(1 Corinthians 6:19-20)

As women, we often think about our appearance. Just listen to our conversations, most of them revolve around being too big, too fat, too much or too something or other.

We are continually plagued by the "what-will-I-wear?" and "how-do-I-look?" questions. After all, our bodies are the temples in which we move around, the visible part of our being in which our hearts and souls dwell and the "I" that other people can see.

Your appearance does indeed matter, we must approach it with love and compassion and we must make an effort to look our best. After all, God made us the crown – the extra special part – of His creation. What we look like and how we feel about our appearance automatically have an effect on our inner being. Looking good gives us the confidence and courage to do our best in all areas of our lives.

> Look after all the aspects of your womanhood. Yes, also cherish and look after your body with compassion. It is one of the most beautiful gifts that your Father gave you.

Help me to care for my body to the best of my abilities, please Creator God. Amen.

Cherish Your Body

The body that is sown is perishable, it is raised imperishable; it is sown in dishonor, it is raised in glory; it is sown in weakness, it is raised in power … (1 Corinthians 15:42-43)

There is a saying that goes: from the moment we are born, we begin to die. This is sad but true in a way, and that is why it is so very important to look after our bodies – as it is the only body we have.

We have to eat healthily, exercise regularly, make sure we get enough rest and keep ourselves from doing things that may harm our bodies. Well, we all know this, we hear it over and over … but it is much easier said than done. And that is because we find ourselves in a modern world where the temptations of fast food, quick-fixes and pick-me-ups keep calling our names. And in addition to that, it is very easy to fall into bad habits for the sake of convenience and comfort.

Taking care of your body is always worth the effort. Self-discipline, regular exercise and healthy eating habits make you a different person, both physically and spiritually. It will make you bloom.

Be good to your body every day.
Then you will feel good about yourself.

Father, please help me to change my lifestyle for the better. Amen.

Hear Him Calling You Back

"He withholds his hand from doing wrong and judges fairly between two parties. He follows My decrees and faithfully keeps My laws. That man is righteous; he will surely live," declares the Sovereign LORD. (Ezekiel 18:8-9)

As children of God, we sometimes feel "out of place". Just like when the Israelites were taken captive to Babylon, an unknown country, because they were disobedient. And of course, our heavenly Father is always deeply disappointed in His children when they wander off.

And that is why He would do anything to get them to turn back to Him. Sometimes by speaking softly to them and other times by allowing disasters, problems and pain in their lives.

Your Father cares deeply for you and will, therefore, allow things to happen to bring you and keep you close to Him. One thing is certain: God always remains faithful, even while He is calling you back to Him. He will always bless obedient children, in spite of trouble, discomfort and sorrow.

Do not lose heart if you don't understand God's ways.
Maybe it is just His way of saying, "Turn back to Me, My child!"

Father, I will follow wherever You may lead. Amen.

Get a Heart Transplant

Create in me a clean heart, O God, and renew a right spirit within me. (Psalm 51:10)

We sometimes need more than just a small heart operation. To be honest, we actually need a heart transplant every single day – we need a totally new heart! A heart that thinks differently, that loves more and that beats with greater passion. Well, fortunately for us our Father's way of doing a heart transplant does not require anesthetic, it is pain free and there are no risks associated with it.

All He asks of us is to grant His Spirit permission to give us a new heart. Because when we allow the Spirit to renew us, a lot of things will change and people will be able to see Christ in the way our hearts beat … how we live.

Pray for a new heart every morning: a heart that is not affected by yesterday's pain. A heart that forgets how other people have wronged you, but that remembers their kindness; a heart that buries anger and resurrects forgiveness; a heart that is positive because negativity is a thing of the past.

Live with the healing, renewing power of the Lord
in your life today. That is true spiritual victory!

Father God, renew me! Make me Your kind of new. Amen.

Manage Anger

Fools give full vent to their rage, but the wise bring calm in the end.
(Proverbs 29:11)

Someone once said that for every minute you are angry, you lose sixty seconds of happiness. Oftentimes, we only spite ourselves by being angry and annoyed.

That is usually when we become unreasonable, when our emotions hold sway over common sense and when we say and do things that we only regret later on. Truth be told, anger makes you weak: it makes you act out of character … because when you are angry, your actions are out of God's will.

There are two ways to break the bad habit of anger. The first is to keep praying and asking the Holy Spirit to control your heart and mind so that you won't lose your temper. And the second, more practical, way to control your anger is to always keep the consequences of an outburst in mind. Because it is as Francis Bacon writes, "Anger is like rain, it breaks itself upon that on which it falls."

Think of how you felt and what it did to you and
the people around you the last time you were angry.
Pray that you will not mar your soul in that way again.

Holy Spirit, please transform the anger in me into forgiving love. Amen.

Weigh Your Words

Peacemakers who sow in peace reap a harvest of righteousness.
(James 3:18)

Sharp words cut people deeply. And don't we know it! How many times have other people's words wounded you? And how many times have your words left others bleeding?

If there is one prayer that we can confidently pray every day, it is: "Lord, please set a strong guard over my big mouth!" Because words that have been spoken cannot be unspoken. People may forgive you for what you have said, but the wounds that you left on their hearts may become scars that stay there for a lifetime. Philip Yancey was quite right when he said that the moment we don't pray about how we speak to people or that we don't pray about how we treat people, something very important is lost in life.

Likewise, words that are positive, constructive and loving also leave a permanent impression on people's lives. The effect of such words on people is that their self-worth is built up, their emotional wounds are healed and they get some peace.

Let's pray that the Holy Spirit will purify and sanctify
our words as we are children of the great God.

Help me, Comforter, to let Your thoughts become my words. Amen.

Manage Your Emotions

The heart of the wise inclines to the right. (Ecclesiastes 10:2)

We all sometimes reach a point in our lives when we feel like running away; when we really don't feel like we can face the world, the people in it or the challenges of life.

Those are the days that our emotions get out of hand, when we blow things out of proportion, when we tend to make irrational assumptions and when we may even make decisions with disastrous consequences. Now, being a woman, you most probably know that you experience these I'm-going-to-lose-it days more or less once a month. That is when other people know that it's best to steer clear of you or to handle you with care.

It is quite human and normal to experience a number of different emotions – even on a single day. But it is also very important that we manage our emotions regardless of how we might be feeling. Because, like Tennyson said, "The happiness of a man in this life does not consist in the absence but in the mastery of his passions."

Let's pray and ask our Creator to enable us
to remain in control of our emotions in all
circumstances ... that He would be in control.

Father, I am pleading for You to give me the grace of self-control. Amen.

OCTOBER 25

Remain Enthusiastic

Come near to God and He will come near to you. (James 4:8)

Enthusiasm is the fire that drives life. It is the power behind our actions, the passion in our efforts and the energy with which we do things. It helps us to overcome obstacles, to persevere in difficult times and to stay courageous. When we have lost our enthusiasm or motivation to do something, we really struggle to keep working on it or to engage with it.

It is also true that the demands that society places on us, constantly receiving bad news and dismal circumstances can suppress our enthusiasm. That is when downheartedness and even depression have a way of slowly creeping up on us.

It is in such times, in particular, that we must draw nearer to God and hold tightly on to His hand so that His goodness can give us a new perspective on things and so that He can once again give us His kind of enthusiasm for life.

Hold tightly to His hand in the grey times of
your life. Then you will feel His colorful
splashes of joy and passion in your heart again.

Help me to live with passion through You, Holy God. Amen.

Reach for the Stars

Those who are wise will shine like the brightness of the heavens, and those who lead many to righteousness, like the stars for ever and ever. (Daniel 12:3)

How much "I can't" do you have in your life? How many times do you hide behind your old way of thinking about the things that you are unable to do. How often do you doubt your own (in)abilities? "I can't" and "I am not …" are negative thoughts that keep you in bondage.

In contrast to that, thinking positive thoughts about your own talents and strengths will give you self-confidence and change your perspective on life completely. The fact of the matter is this: you were born with a great number of unique characteristics; precious treasures that were placed inside you by the Creator so that you can discover them, develop them and make the most of them. You will be capable of doing anything if you focus on personal development and concentrate on your best qualities.

Then you will be able to look past the limitations that you and others have placed on you over the years. You will outdo yourself by using those things that you already have to make your dream a reality.

Start the day with an "I can" attitude and see
how the stars move closer and closer to you.

Spirit of Life, help me to be the best me. Amen.

Visualize Your Funeral

The path of the righteous is like the morning sun, shining ever brighter till the full light of day. (Proverbs 4:18)

Eulogies at funerals always say the most beautiful things about the person that passed away. Quite often we only hear of a person's good qualities when he or she is no longer with us.

What do you think people will say about you at your funeral one day? Will they talk about your successes, your achievements and all the goals you achieved? Or do you think they'll talk about the kind of person that you were? The difference you made to their lives? The way you lived?

What would you want them to say? Only you know. Because only you know what your deepest desires, dreams and expectations are.

One thing is true: if your life is illuminated by Christ's light, your legacy will be different from that of someone who lived their life in darkness – no matter what your achievements were here on earth!

Lord Jesus, be in me so that I can illuminate the world with Your holiness. Amen.

Honor Him with Your Life

For though we live in the world, we do not wage war as the world does. (2 Corinthians 10:3)

Do you think that your life – who you are and what you do – glorifies God? Can you confidently say that you are helping to expand the Kingdom of God?

Regardless of what you do for a living or what your calling is, you are always in your Father's service if you are a child of God. Just like Jesus said in John 15:16-17: "I chose you and appointed you … This is My command: Love each other."

When you honor God with your life, there is the danger that the Evil One will try to stop you from glorifying his enemy. And so you will see that the more you honor God, the more the Evil One will attack you.

> Ask the Holy Spirit to equip you every day so that you can glorify God with your whole life. Do that, stand strong and know: God helps you!

Help me to live my life in such a way that it glorifies You every day, great God. Amen.

Make the World a Better Place

"I will give them an undivided heart and put a new spirit in them; I will remove from them their heart of stone and give them a heart of flesh." (Ezekiel 11:19)

We often live only for ourselves. And so our world and most of our dreams, thoughts and even our prayers revolve only around our own lives.

If we are honest with ourselves, we will have to admit that we often have a Cain attitude that asks wordlessly: "Am I my brother's/neighbor's/colleague's keeper?" The truth is: we are! You and I are there to make a real difference in the lives of the people around us; we must help them to draw nearer to God and to reach their full potential.

So, ask yourself this question today: does the way I live my life and how I interact with and support other people make a positive difference?

Serving God means that we must make the world a better
place through the way we live our lives. So, ask yourself:
How can I make a positive impact with what I do?

Father God, use me in the lives of those around me, please. Amen.

OCTOBER 30

He Will Always Love You

"On the day when I act," says the LORD Almighty, "they will be My trea-sured possession. I will spare them, just as a father has compassion and spares his son who serves him." (Malachi 3:17)

When things don't go your way, does it mean that God is no longer holding you in the faithful palm of His hand? Or that He is angry with you? No. God is not out to get you or to cause you pain. Quite the opposite, everything He does is to show you how very much He loves you.

The book of Malachi tells us how God's people were stunned when things didn't go the way they expected them to. And then they queried God, like all of us would. But then we hear His answer: "I love you very much …" In spite of the fact that the people did not behave the way God wanted them to, His love for them knows no bounds.

All He asks of them (and us) is to do the right thing and that their love for Him must be genuine.

Your Father loves you, in spite of …

Please hold me tightly today, Lord. Amen.

Build an Altar for God

There he set up an altar and called it El Elohe Israel [El is the God of Israel or mighty is the God of Israel]. (Genesis 33:20)

Faith is to know God as your personal Savior, to love Him and to know that He is your Father and your God. Yes, faith means that you acknowledge Him as the Author of everything in your life, the One who guides you, gives you breakthroughs and who will never forsake you.

The wonderful thing about having faith in your heart is that the Spirit of God Himself placed it there. So, if you have faith, it is pure grace.

Have you ever genuinely thanked the Father for picking you to be His child? For the fact that He called you and made you His own so that you can live with Him for all eternity? Build an altar of thanksgiving in your heart today.

Just thank Him for His indescribable goodness in your life and tell Him again: Lord, I believe! I worship, praise and thank You for loving me so very much. And therefore Lord, I want to and will witness for You.

Thank You, God, for helping me to be a sincere believer. Amen.

November

The Courage to Persevere

"May you reach your goal, the finish line, with your torch still burning! The highest honor one can receive is to have someone say of you: 'she remained faithful and sincere to the end!'"

~ William Barclay

You need to persevere so that when you have done the will of God, you will receive what He has promised.

~ Hebrews 10:36

Hang in There

... [you] who through faith are shielded by God's power until the coming of the salvation that is ready to be revealed in the last time.
(1 Peter 1:5)

It has never been and probably will never be easy to hang in there. Especially when we don't want to hang in there anymore, when we're sick and tired of our life. The same old routine every day, getting up early and doing our daily stint, dealing with complicated relationships, the constant battle to stick to a budget ... or simply the struggle to face the world with a fake smile – it all just gets too much at times.

It's quite normal to feel like you've had enough as the year draws to an end. But may the devotionals of this month help you to take heart and find strength to hang in there. A good start is to tell God exactly how you're feeling. Tell Him all about your struggle, your battle to remain positive and your utter exhaustion. Be open and honest and share your heart with the Holy Spirit who is with you so that He can meet your specific needs.

Know that God is holding you close – particularly
in the times when you have had enough.

Lord, help me. I don't want to carry on and I can't carry on! Amen.

Be like Daniel

My God sent His angel, and he shut the mouths of the lions. They have not hurt me. (Daniel 6:22)

We know Daniel as the man in the lions' den: the man that was thrown into a den with hungry lions because of his faith, but who got out of the predicament without so much as a scratch due to God's grace. Daniel should, however, be remembered for much more than just the lions' den episode … because this man showed us what real courage is in so many different ways.

Daniel and his friends lived in difficult times. They were taken captive as young men and then they had to live as exiles in Babylon, where they faced numerous challenges. Time after time, their faith and faithfulness to God were tested, like when they were ordered to deny their faith while being threatened with death. And every time they chose – in spite of the death threats – to remain absolutely faithful to their God. And time after time, the Lord saved them from the jaws of death in miraculous ways.

Let's pray that God will give us the courage to never deny Him; to stay faithful to Him even though we are pressured.

Faithful Father, please give me the courage to remain absolutely faithful to You. Amen.

Live Healthily

At the end of the ten days they looked healthier and better nourished than any of the young men who ate the royal food. (Daniel 1:15)

It really is not easy to always maintain a healthy lifestyle. Particularly at this time of the year when year-end functions, Christmas dinners and holiday plans are served up next to our end-of-the-year busyness. We, however, also know that bad habits, unhealthy eating and an unbalanced lifestyle all have a way of catching up with you. And then we not only feel terrible, but we also struggle to be at our best.

When Daniel landed in King Nebuchadnezzar's palace so many years ago, he was also tempted to eat the rich royal food and drink of the king's wine. But Daniel and his friends made a choice to do things differently. They decided to eat only vegetables and drink only water. And ten days later, everyone was surprised at how much healthier and stronger Daniel and his friends looked in comparison with the other young men.

You and I need to make healthy choices in order to function optimally. Choose to follow a healthy and balanced lifestyle, even at this time of the year. It is always worth it!

Guide of my life, my flesh is weak. Please help me. Amen.

Look for His Guidance

Daniel replied, "No wise man, enchanter, magician or diviner can explain to the king the mystery he has asked about, but there is a God in heaven who reveals mysteries ..." (Daniel 2:27-28)

King Nebuchadnezzar was feeling very frustrated. He had had a strange dream and none of his "wise" men were able to interpret the dream for him – and then Daniel heard about it and asked God to reveal the meaning of the dream to him. Yes, because Daniel's ear was finely tuned into God's voice, he was able to understand the things that no one else could.

Are you as finely tuned into God's voice as Daniel was? Do you take the time to spend quiet time with the Lord every day? Do you allow Him to fill you with His Spirit so that you can hear what He tells you during the day and so that you can do what He asks?

When you are tuned into God, your entire life will play a part in His symphony. Then your life will harmonize with God's will and you will be able to do things that no one else can.

Pray throughout the day today and ask His
Spirit to guide you in everything that you do.

Guide me today ... every day, please Holy Spirit. Amen.

NOVEMBER 5

Say "No"

If we are thrown into the blazing furnace, the God we serve is able to deliver us from it, and He will deliver us from Your Majesty's hand. But even if He does not, we want you to know, Your Majesty, that we will not serve your gods or worship the image of gold you have set up. (Daniel 3:17-18)

It is not always easy to resist temptation when "everyone is doing it" or when we are expected to take part in things that run counter to your principles. Because saying "no" takes an awful lot of courage – whether it has to do with our own lives, our jobs or the upbringing of our children.

Daniel's friends, Shadrach, Meshach and Abednego's refusal to worship the manmade gods of the king spelt certain death for them. And yet they decided to stick to their principles, in spite of the fact that it meant that they would be thrown into a fiery furnace. They were determined to serve only their God … even in the face of death.

May you also have the courage to say "no" to the wrong things, because with that you give God a convincing "yes".

Lord, help me to do what You ask. Amen.

Warn Others

"Therefore, Your Majesty, be pleased to accept my advice: renounce your sins by doing what is right, and your wickedness by being kind to the oppressed. It may be that then your prosperity will continue."
(Daniel 4:27)

Some people just don't want to listen. Even though they've had someone warn them before and even though they are aware that they are digging their own grave, they simply keep doing the wrong things. Just like King Nebuchadnezzar. Despite the fact that Daniel told him exactly what was going to happen to him if he did not heed God's warning, he continued on his journey of self-glorification … without God.

We all know someone who is on the wrong path which leads to self-destruction. The fact that it may be difficult to talk to that person or that he or she may not want to hear it, should not keep us from trying. God places people around us for a reason. Some of them are in our lives so that we can carefully lead them back to the right path.

Carefully listen to what God is telling you. Let Him
tell you who is in need of a warning. Also allow Him
to teach you how to admonish someone in love.

I am at Your service, Savior, use me as You please. Amen.

Speak to God All Day Long

Now when Daniel learned that the decree had been published, he went home to his upstairs room where the windows opened toward Jerusalem. Three times a day he got down on his knees and prayed, giving thanks to his God, just as he had done before. (Daniel 6:10)

How often do you pray? Every now and then, twice a day … or the whole time? Prayer should never feel like a heavy burden of duty, because prayer is the wonderful privilege to speak to your Father, to hear His voice and to find rest in Him. And you can pray about anything, anytime, anywhere.

The wonderful thing is that once you have gotten into the habit of continually communicating with the Holy Spirit, you can no longer live without constantly doing it. Isn't it nice to know you have Someone who will listen to you without judging you, who loves you unconditionally and who has all the advice in the world to offer you? Like Charles Spurgeon said, you cannot stumble if you are on your knees.

God blesses His faithful-in-prayer friends – are you one of them?

I want You with me all day every day, Friend of my life, please stay with me. Amen.

Go Against the Flow

Then these men went as a group and found Daniel praying and asking God for help. (Daniel 6:11)

It is sometimes necessary to go against the flow. Especially when you are expected to do things that run counter to your values and principles. Or when others want you to renounce your Father. That is when God expects you to swim against the everyone-is-doing-it current.

And that is exactly what Daniel did when King Darius issued a decree that ordered everyone to worship only him for 30 days. That is when Daniel showed his true colors, even more so than before. He made very sure that everyone saw that he was going against the flow of the lie by praying to his God three times a day.

Even though he ran the risk of being thrown in the lions' den, he openly and without hesitation continued to do what he knew to be right. Now, that is persevering in faith!

God protects and rewards His obedient and faithful children in extraordinary and surprising ways. May you have the courage to also go against the flow when needed.

God of wisdom, teach me to stand up for what is right. Amen.

Enjoy His Compassion

The LORD make His face shine on you and be gracious to you; the LORD turn His face toward you and give you peace.
(Numbers 6:25-26)

It is easy to think that God is an angry, judgmental God and that makes us afraid of being in His presence. The truth, however, is that God looks at us with the greatest love and compassion in His eyes, because He loves each one of His children unconditionally.

And because He is good, He makes all that He is and all that He has available to us. His wisdom, power, love, peace, greatness, comfort and blessing are all at our disposal. He is literally standing ready to give it all to us in abundance. If only we would ask Him for it, listen to Him and share everything about our lives with Him.

Your Master wants you to turn your heart to Him throughout the day and night so that He can assure you that you are precious in His sight and that He, therefore, wants to take care of you and bless you.

Thank You, Lord, for having compassion on me. Amen.

Learn to Pray

Be ... faithful in prayer. (Romans 12:12)

Now, you might be wondering why you need to "learn" to pray if it is the most natural thing for humans to do. It is necessary to learn so that you can make the most of prayer – so that you can use and enjoy this precious gift from God to the full.

There are numerous books on prayer patterns, body posture and techniques. And yet there are only a few basic rules that one must follow. William Barclay gives us the following guidelines:

- Always be honest. Like Martin Luther said, "Don't lie to God."
- Be straightforward. Real prayer requires honest self-reflection and searching your own heart.
- Be unselfish. God will never grant selfish requests.
- Trust in God. He sees the bigger picture – that is why only He knows what is best.
- Pray and work. God will not do for us what we can do for ourselves.
- Pray within the laws of nature. Prayer cannot overturn natural laws.

> Sincere prayer not only changes the
> world, it also changes your heart.

O Spirit, please teach me how to pray ... pray for me. Amen.

Enjoy Him

Be joyful in hope, patient in affliction, faithful in prayer.
(Romans 12:12)

God is closer to us than our own breath! He is in us and part of us … so we can just enjoy His glorious closeness. Yes, His Holy Spirit wants to caress us with His comfort, cuddle us with His calm and generously give us His divine gifts. So, God doesn't require well-prepared and well-formulated prayers before He grants us His presence. He just wants to do it because He loves us so much.

Of course it's good to pour your heart out to God, but the most fulfilling moments in prayer is when we just sit at His feet, being totally dependent on Him and without having a list of requests … when we are not afraid and have no reservations about being with Him. It is in these times of just being with Him that God reveals to us who He really is. And then we can hear Him say, "I am with you."

> Make time today – every day – to sit on your Father's lap like a young child so that He can wrap His arms around you and whisper softly in your ear, "I love you so much!"

Here I am, Father. Here I am. Amen.

Wait for His Time

*This is what the Lord says: "In the time of My favor I will answer you,
and in the day of salvation I will help you; I will keep you."*
(Isaiah 49:8)

Have you ever felt like God was just not hearing your prayers? Why have you been praying about this one thing for so long without getting an answer from Him? Why does He sometimes respond to our requests with "No" and at other times with "Wait"? Yes, even great believers sometimes wrestle with God about so-called unanswered prayers.

The answer to these questions lies in the fact that God's thoughts are all-encompassing. The picture He sees is much bigger than our existence, our small world and our earthly time zones. He, who is the Alpha and Omega, sees every person and every situation in a heavenly context and from a heavenly perspective.

He sees your yesterdays and tomorrows. So, it is best just to pray as Johann Wolfgang von Goethe did: O Lord, let not my desire come to pass, but what is right in Your sight.

God will answer your prayers in His perfect
time and way. Just stay faithful in prayer.

Thank You, heavenly God, that I know You know! Help me to wait patiently for Your answer. Amen.

Pray to Your Father

"But when you pray, go into your room, close the door and pray to your Father, who is unseen. Then your Father, who sees what is done in secret, will reward you." (Matthew 6:6)

It's true that many people who pray the Lord's Prayer on Sundays, spend their week living as though they are orphans. And that is so unnecessary! There is no reason for us not to continuously speak to our Father.

Yes, prayer is actually the most natural thing for humans to do. And as children of the living God, we have the wonderful privilege of constantly conversing with the Lord. His Holy Spirit is always standing ready to bring us relief in our struggles, to give us peace in the place of our worry, to help us resist temptation and to assure us of His love and faithfulness.

You don't have to live like a Christian orphan. Your Father is with you all day. Share your heart with Him without ceasing.

O Lord, thank You that I can trust You without reservation. Amen.

Keep Being His Witness

While they were stoning him, Stephen prayed, "Lord Jesus, receive my spirit." (Acts 7:59)

We might live in a country where we have freedom of religion, where we can worship and witness about our Lord without hesitation and fear. But what if it was different? Would we have had the courage, like Stephen, to remain faithful even unto death?

Can we say in all honesty that we are – even in our daily lives – our Father's faithful witnesses every day? Yes, it is not always easy to stand firm in the faith. But that is exactly what God expects of His children: to remain faithful to Him even unto death! Because that is when He will demonstrate His faithfulness through His grace.

Remember Vance Havner who said that one man with a genuine glowing experience with God is worth more than a library full of arguments.

May you receive the grace never to be afraid or ashamed
because of the God you serve. May you be an audible
and visible testimony of your God every day.

Give me the courage to always say "yes" to You, Father. Amen.

Take Back Lost Time

Instead, you ought to say, "If it is the Lord's will, we will live and do this or that." (James 4:15)

One of the reasons why we feel sick and tired of it all at the end of the year is that our lives get ahead of us. Everything seems to be happening all at once and the fast pace of our lives forces us to just keep going and going. The very last thing on our list of priorities is quiet time! And that is why we often tend to neglect our soul-and-Word time.

Dear friend, if life keeps you so busy that you start to lose yourself, you are right where Satan wants you. He wants to keep you away from yourself, from others and from God most of all. So, be aware of this and know that now is the time to resist the Evil One's schemes to lure you away from God.

Therefore, be sure to make time – now more than ever – to listen for your Father's voice, to pour your heart out to Him and to draw strength from His inexhaustible source.

Turn your back on the world's noise and let your heart have quiet time with the Spirit – who is already waiting for you.

Spirit of God, help me to refuse to go along with a life that tends to get too busy … so that I can find You again. Amen.

Stay on Course

In all this you greatly rejoice, though now for a little while you may have had to suffer grief in all kinds of trials. These have come so that the proven genuineness of your faith – of greater worth than gold, which perishes even though refined by fire – may result in praise, glory and honor when Jesus Christ is revealed. (1 Peter 1:6-7)

Nowhere in the Bible or in history does it say that it is easy to persevere in the faith. On the contrary, the more we study the Scriptures, the lives of other believers as well as our own life, the clearer it becomes that our walk of faith is full of roundabouts, turnoffs, steep hills and even barricades.

We need to be aware of this. Otherwise we will easily become despondent in the face of opposition, lose hope when we fall spiritually or just throw in the towel. Peter makes it very clear that our faith will be tested through trials. But he also encourages us not to be put off when confronted with barricades on our faith walk. In other words, he is saying that when you fall, get back up; if you've taken a wrong turn, then turn back and if you have wandered off, get back on track.

Don't allow anything to make you veer off your faith-course. Keep your eyes on Christ. See Christ's return in your mind's eye and stay on course – no matter what. God will help you!

Faithful Father, forgive me for when I am like a runaway child and then bring me back – back to You. Amen.

Be like Gold

These have come so that the proven genuineness of your faith – of greater worth than gold, which perishes even though refined by fire – may result in praise, glory and honor when Jesus Christ is revealed. (1 Peter 1:7)

"My friend, I am tired of holding on!" I said to one of my dear friends just the other day. Yes, we all go through times when we know that we need to push on and keep our heads up, but when we just don't want to anymore, because we are exhausted from putting up a fight ... tired of keeping our courage up.

Peter wrote this letter shortly before he died as a martyr. In spite of his own struggle, he is encouraging the believers to keep on doing God's will and to live out love – even when the world becomes like a fiery furnace.

Dear heart, if you are also tired of holding on, then you are most probably finding yourself in the crucible of life – where God is purifying you even more. Stay faithful to Him even in the furnace of refinement. He will surely reward you richly!

Great God, make me faithful ... to the end. Amen.

Help Each Other

Confess your sins to each other and pray for each other so that you may be healed. The earnest prayer of a righteous person has great power and produces wonderful results. (James 5:16)

Our dear Father knows our hearts. He knows how easily we veer off course and He has understanding of our human weaknesses and emotions. And that is also why God gave us one another. He did not intend for us to fight the battle on earth all on our own.

That is why He gave us fellow believers in our walk of faith: people who will pick us up when we fall, who will encourage us when we can't carry on and who will pray for us. Always pray for and with your fellow-believer friends. Ask them what their prayer requests are on a regular basis and then bring it before the throne on their behalf. Also be willing to ask others to pray for you.

Ask them to help you get through every challenge by interceding for you. We are meant to support one another in this way so that we can set the example that God expects us to right to the end.

Reach out to other believers and strengthen one another through prayer. It makes the road so much more bearable!

Help me to be a friend who really cares, Father, and give me friends who will pray for me as well. Amen.

Keep Working on Relationships

But when He, the Spirit of truth, comes, He will guide you into all the truth. (John 16:13)

It's no joke to maintain healthy relationships when we feel tired, irritated and stressed out. At this time of year, it is very easy for misunderstandings to find their way into our relationships as most of us are suffering from an overload of emotions. And the more we struggle to get along with one another, the more stressed and tired we feel.

Today, ask the Spirit to come and renew you completely – even though you may feel all worked up. Ask Him to remove all negativity, all preconceived ideas and all disparaging emotions from your heart. Then ask Him to come into your life and to come and purify every single part of who you are with His love.

When you have Him by your side, you will have all the wisdom, courage and strength you need to handle every relationship in your life in a positive way.

O Lord, change the world ... and begin with me.

O Father, I don't always want to be compliant and turn the other cheek. Please give me some of Your grace. Amen.

Get Up Again

[I am] persecuted, but not abandoned; struck down, but not destroyed. (2 Corinthians 4:9)

If there is one person who knew how to get back up time after time, it is Paul. While his body was wasting away, his spiritual life went from strength to strength. In times when he felt like he didn't know what to do, God blessed him with boundless wisdom and courage. When he was persecuted by people, God never abandoned him and when life knocked him down, the Spirit put him back on his feet again. Paul was only able to hang in there because the Holy Spirit helped him to.

God never leaves believers to their fate. He assures us of His faithfulness, support and grace again and again. He renews our inner being every day – He makes us new so that we can stand up again; He makes us new so that we can look life squarely in the eyes; He makes us new so that we have courage for every day and so that we can stick it out… no matter what.

Take God on His Word today and live with hope.

Thank You for being a God who cares for people even if they fall. Thank You for being my God today as well. Amen.

Roller Coaster Emotions

I have learned the secret of being content in any and every situation, whether well fed or hungry, whether living in plenty or in want. (Philippians 4:12)

Sometimes it's hard to understand ourselves! Because the one day we're on cloud nine and the next ... we're down in the dumps. And then there are those times that we feel negative about doing something, just to be pleasantly surprised with how positive the event turns out to be. Yes, as women we are very good at experiencing up-and-down emotions.

The fact of the matter is: life has good and bad, nice and nasty, excitement and boredom, happiness as well as pain and victory along with defeat. We can glean from Paul's letters that he was also intensely aware of the contrasts in life. This hero of the faith, however, knew exactly how to turn an upside-down situation right side up again. He taught us how to live our lives with success and suffering, praise and rejection, love and sorrow being in harmony.

Paul was able to ride the roller coaster of life
because he had God by his side, and you do too!

Lord, give me the ability to live my life in such a way that others will see You in me, always and in all circumstances. Amen.

More than Just Survival

No, I strike a blow to my body and make it my slave so that after I have preached to others, I myself will not be disqualified for the prize. (1 Corinthians 9:27)

Do you also sometimes feel like you are just barely surviving? Like you have just enough energy to drag yourself through the day every day. If you feel despondent about your bleak life, you might find some of Paul's truths about life helpful:

- Paul made very sure that his knowledge about God was thorough and pure. And that is why he was able to recall it in difficult times.
- When he felt like God had deserted him, he just pleaded for mercy again. And that is why the Spirit was always there for him to guide him through such times.
- He praised the Lord even in times of suffering. That is how he showed God to the world.
- He reminded himself that every situation would come to an end. And that is why he always seemed to have courage and why he was able to carry on.

Pray and ask the Holy Spirit to give you the ability,
the wisdom and courage to handle every situation
gracefully and with faith. Hold on, dear heart!

O Spirit of God, teach me how to do more than just survive. Amen.

Look Past Today

Not that I have already obtained all this, or have already arrived at my goal, but I press on to take hold of that for which Christ Jesus took hold of me. (Philippians 3:12)

All our lives revolve only around today. Everything we think, talk about and do relates to our life here on earth and making it – the here and now – better.

Yes, we are mostly focused on the life-steps that we walk here on earth, while what happens after we've crossed the finish line seems to be of no importance to us. And yet we only live for about seventy or so years on earth (if we're lucky, that is) … while we're going to spend an eternity in heaven.

Maybe we should take some time and seriously consider what our lives revolve around. Maybe our focus is completely wrong and maybe that is why we are so unhappy.

Keep your eyes on the finish line (the hereafter) today.
It will make your present a lot more meaningful as well!

Lord, I want to take every step of my life so that it glorifies You. Help me to live in today while keeping tomorrow in mind. Amen.

Make God Happy

The Holy Spirit descended on Him in bodily form like a dove. And a voice came from heaven: "You are My Son, whom I love; with You I am well pleased." (Luke 3:22)

When God created you, He had a wonderful plan with your life. He could already see how you would glorify Him with your life. And today – even though you have disappointed Him so many times – He still knows how you will glorify Him.

His Holy Spirit is there every day to help you reach God's goal with your life. All you need to do is to stay tuned into His voice and to obediently do what He asks you to.

The wonderful thing is that when we live our lives in a way that makes God happy, we also receive peace and fulfillment in abundance ourselves.

Pray that you will live your life according to God's will every day so that when you reach the finish line one day, you will hear: well done! Your life made God sing for joy!

May my life bring joy to You, Father. Amen.

Live with Hope

"Do not let your hearts be troubled. You believe in God; believe also in Me." (John 14:1)

There are two prerequisites for success in life. The first is to have a destination in mind when you start out: "To Canaan!" The second is to keep going on the road you started out on: "After you arrived in Canaan," said Berton Brayley.

As children of God we are on our way to our Canaan: that eternal glorious place overflowing with milk and honey. We have God leading the way with His pillar of cloud and pillar of fire, we have His Spirit with us and Jesus telling us: "Take heart!" And that is why we can live with so much hope; hope that knows that our triune God is with us every step of our journey and hope that knows, in particular, that we are on our way to our eternal home.

> Just keep going. Do not throw in the towel. And
> don't ever doubt. You are safe in the palm on
> His hand and you are making your way to a
> glorious life of happiness; a life of eternal hope!

Father of hope, help me to complete the journey You mapped out for me. Amen.

NOVEMBER 26

Be Out on the Track

"Therefore go and make disciples of all nations, baptizing them in the name of the Father and of the Son and of the Holy Spirit."
(Matthew 28:19)

It's very easy to sit on the side lines and criticize others. Just listen to the clever advice that men dish out while watching the match on TV. And how quick are we to point out someone else's weaknesses? Maybe it is a fear of being criticized that make many of us decide to rather sit in the stands, doing nothing, while we look on as other believers run around the racetrack of life.

God does not want His children to sit in the stands and not live out their faith. He wants energetic, enthusiastic participants who won't hesitate to participate and be on His team. He wants people who are willing to run out onto the racetrack of life and who will run their hearts out in the race of faith so as to win even more athletes for the Kingdom.

Where are you? Are you sitting in
the stands or are you in the race?

Give me the courage to be an active disciple in Your service, please Lord.
Amen.

Overcome Obstacles

Consider it pure joy, my brothers and sisters, whenever you face trials of many kinds, because you know that the testing of your faith produces perseverance. (James 1:2-3)

A blowfly can't actually fly! The weight of its wings in relation to its body makes it, aerodynamically and mathematically speaking, simply impossible to fly. Fortunately, the blowfly does not know this and therefore … it flies!

How do you see your life, responsibilities and your faith? Do you only ever notice all the reasons for why something can't be done? Do the big and small obstacles in your life-path often cause you to stumble and fall … and stay down? Or are you so motivated that you just keep going – in spite of everything that weighs you down – that you just persevere and never lose heart.

Hold tightly to Christ's hand in times when you are faced with obstacles, difficulties and when you get tired. He is there to help you get through or over any obstacle. Then you can look back and know: in spite of … I flew!

Dear friend, go and fly today! Because with Him … you can!

Almighty Father, I put my trust in You every moment of every day, because You can do everything! Amen.

Put His Word First

Submit yourselves, then, to God. (James 4:7)

Do you feel overwhelmed by all the information in the media and social media? It is as if you are always a step or two behind, because before you know it there is yet another source of information and you have your children excitedly telling you all about the latest gadget or newest app.

Relax! You don't have to know about everything that goes on in the world and technological savvy never got anyone into heaven. There is only one place where we can find all the answers to life's important questions … and that is in the Word of God. If you read the Scriptures on a regular basis, you'll find everything you need to know. And that the truths that His Word and His Spirit teach us are always at the forefront of being human.

Make time to devour the timeless Word of God
and allow the Holy Spirit to lead you into the future.
Then you will never be uninformed.

Master, teach me the truths contained in Your Word as well as the wisdom of Your Spirit … every day! Amen.

Never Lose Courage

"Look, I am coming soon! My reward is with Me, and I will give to each person according to what they have done." (Revelation 22:12)

It is the end of November. You are exhausted and you are counting down the days to the end of the year. Yes, at this time of the year all we have to do is to survive … to persevere. May the following encouraging words help you to keep going in the final stretch of this year's race:

- Louis Pasteur said, "Let me tell you the secret that has led me to my goal. My strength lies solely in my tenacity."
- Samuel Johnson wrote that: "Great works are performed not by strength but by perseverance."
- Charles Spurgeon said, "By perseverance the snail reached the ark."
- And Christ? He says, "Look, I am coming soon!"

> May the knowledge that the Spirit will give you
> the strength to persevere until Christ returns, give
> you the courage and strength you need for the last
> round. Hang in there, dear heart, you can!

Lord, please be my strength, my power, my perseverance. Amen.

Take Him with You

The Lord replied, "My Presence will go with you, and I will give you rest." Then Moses said to Him, "If Your Presence does not go with us, do not send us up from here." (Exodus 33:14-15)

During their journey through the wilderness, God showed the Israelites that He is faithful time after time. And time after time, they turned their backs on Him and worshiped worthless idols. And then God's man, Moses, had to intercede with God on the people's behalf … as well as help the people to continue on their journey with God by their side.

Without God, life is nothing but a failure. With God, life and death is a success. Know this today: you may not tackle one day of your life on your own. Life is just too hard and cruel without God's love and protection.

Ask God to accompany you on your journey through life every day. You will feel Him reassuring you just like He assured Moses: "I will do the very thing you have asked, because I am pleased with you and I know you by name" (Exod. 33:17).

Father of grace, here I am. Vulnerable, scared and small. Please guide me every day for the rest of my life. Amen.

December

The Courage to Kneel Down

"As we grow old, the beauty steals inward."

~ Ralph Waldo Emerson

*"For God so loved the world that He gave His one and only Son,
that whoever believes in Him shall not perish but have eternal life."*

~ John 3:16

Live to the Full

... and to know this love that surpasses knowledge – that you may be filled to the measure of all the fullness of God. (Ephesians 3:19)

December usually comes with more than the normal share of emotions. We are drawing near to the end of a long road, we are tired and busier than usual. Truth be told, all we want to do is to pack our suitcases, find a quiet beach where nothing and no one can bother us and relax …

But now, we can't! We still need to get through the last rush of the year, gracefully. And on top of that, there are vacation plans that need to be finalized and family gatherings that need to be organized.

Will this be another December where feelings run high and where things just don't work out the way you had hoped? Or are you going to approach things differently this year?

> The choice is yours. You may not have control over everything that comes your way this month … but you certainly have control over the way that you are going to handle it.

Father, I kneel down before You. Please teach me how to enjoy life to the full – in spite of everything. Amen.

DECEMBER 2

Now Is the Time to Kneel

"But I have been the LORD your God ever since you came out of Egypt. You shall acknowledge no God but Me, no Savior except Me."
(Hosea 13:4)

We are utterly exhausted! The days are too short, time is running out and there are still a thousand-and-one things that need to get done. When we are so caught up in the hurry-scurry, we struggle to make time for prayer, Bible study and quiet time.

Life is simply too busy right now. If you feel like this, you need to call a halt immediately. When you no longer have time to spend with your Father, because your life has gotten away from you, now is the time – more than ever – to go and kneel before Him. Plan your day, move appointments and do whatever it takes to kneel before your Lord on a regular basis.

That is where you will find rest for your unsettled soul, strength to face another day and courage to shoulder all the responsibilities.

> Do not lose courage. Especially not the
> courage to spend quiet time with Him.

Master of my life, forgive me for wandering off and please bring me back to Your throne, to where I want to kneel … want to stay. Amen.

DECEMBER 3

Live for Today and for Tomorrow

So we fix our eyes not on what is seen, but on what is unseen, since what is seen is temporary, but what is unseen is eternal.
(2 Corinthians 4:18)

As Christians, we need to strike a fine balance between our earthly and heavenly lives. After all, we know that our life here on earth is just temporary and that we are merely passing through on our way to our eternal home. And therefore, it is easy to fall into the "just-come-Lord-Jesus" syndrome.

However, God really wants us to live every day to the full. Peter concludes his second letter with a wonderful message as he writes: "But grow in the grace and knowledge of our Lord and Savior Jesus Christ. To Him be glory both now and forever!" (2 Pet. 3:18).

So today, go and express God's grace towards other people. Show the world what His loving goodness looks like and share His message of hope with others. That is how to live for today and for every tomorrow of your life.

Master of my heart, show me how to live for You. Teach me the art of establishing a piece of heaven here on earth. Amen.

Know That He Is There

Whether you turn to the right or to the left, your ears will hear a voice behind you, saying, "This is the way; walk in it." (Isaiah 30:21)

Do you sometimes also wish that God would just send you an email, text message or a letter? That He would send little notes that suggest possible solutions to your problems, that give you the answers to all your questions and that tell you exactly what you have to do, what you need to decide and where you need to go. Wouldn't that be nice?

However, our omniscient Creator knew that He could not do things that way. He is only there to guide us and then He leaves the decisions up to us.

God does not send us emails and cryptic messages. He gives us much more than that. He gives us His Word and His Spirit to point us in the right direction, to help us along the way and to bring us back on track when we have wandered off. You can be sure that He is there. Seek Him out and put your trust in Him.

Spirit of God, I worship Your greatness. Thank You for never leaving me alone and that I, therefore, have courage to face every day. Amen.

Open Your Heart

We prove ourselves by our purity, our understanding, our patience, our kindness, by the Holy Spirit within us, and by our sincere love.
(2 Corinthians 6:6)

The contrast between rich and poor is never quite as obvious as during holiday and Christmas times. While some people are relaxing in luxurious holiday homes, others are crammed into shacks wondering where their next meal is going to come from.

While we are spending time with family and friends sitting around tables stacked high with food, others struggle to survive. Some people are all alone wondering if there is anyone out there who loves them, who really cares about them.

Of course, you and I cannot meet everyone's needs at this time of year. But maybe we can brighten up just one person's life this Christmas season. Maybe we should share some of Jesus' love with someone who least expects it.

Pray and ask the Holy Spirit to show you who you can
make a difference to this year. Then go and do it.

Open my eyes, Lord, and show me how and to whom to give. Amen.

Kneel Next to Others

Rather, in humility value others above yourselves, not looking to your own interests but each of you to the interests of the others.
(Philippians 2:3-4)

People have different needs. There are those that have a great need for material things, but then there are also those who desperately want something else. They are the ones who don't know true love or who are walking around with broken, hurting or rejected hearts; the ones who are sick or the ones who have lost all hope.

There are people with empty, longing hearts in every single community. There are thousands who have never heard of Jesus' love for them. There are also those who yearn for attention, a patient ear or a sympathetic shoulder to cry on. Others desperately need just someone who will be there for them, maybe pray for them or tell them: "You are precious in God's sight. How can I help you?"

Where, how and next to whom do you think you should kneel this season? To whose heart can you bring comfort and hope? Pray that the Holy Spirit will give you the courage to go out and do it.

Lord Jesus, show me where to go and be Your hands and feet in this time. Amen.

Be His Disciple

Preach the Word; be prepared in season and out of season; correct, rebuke and encourage – with great patience and careful instruction. (2 Timothy 4:2)

There are times in any Christian's life when he or she feels unwelcome and uncomfortable. Like when your colleagues' conversations and use of language jar with your morals, when others want to do things that you don't agree with or when the world expects you to just go with the flow. That is when we are called to openly serve the Lord above all. That is when we need to show who we will bow down to: the world or our God?

Remember the instruction that Paul gave Timothy when he wrote the following in his letter: If others spread nonsense, then set them straight. If they don't want to listen, then rebuke them. When someone has lost hope, encourage them. Be patient when helping people to understand the things of God all the better (2 Tim. 4:2, paraphrased).

May you always have the courage to
show the world who your Father is.

Faithful God, help me to never deny You! Help me to be a faithful servant of Yours. Amen.

Kneel Again

He has caused His wonders to be remembered; the LORD is gracious and compassionate. (Psalm 111:4)

Sin and feelings of guilt and shame have a way of keeping us off our knees. After all, no one likes to appear before the Father when they know that they have done something that was against His will.

It doesn't matter if we fell into temptation, or if we behaved incorrectly or neglected to do something. We would rather just stay away from Him because we feel embarrassed, so we try to stand on our own … but then we fall down in any case.

Don't allow feelings of guilt to keep you off your knees. Because that is precisely when you need to go and kneel before your Father. He is waiting for you. Yes, He will never push His children who have true repentant hearts away. He knows that we are not perfect, that we make mistakes, that we often fail. That is exactly why He sent His Son to the world – the Child that came so that all our sins can be forgiven.

> God wants to offer you His forgiveness.
> So, give all your sin to Him and be sure
> of this: He has already redeemed you!

Thank You, great God, for forgiving me time after time and for loving me unconditionally. Amen.

Do Not Doubt

"Blessed is anyone who does not stumble on account of Me."
(Matthew 11:6)

The world has all kinds of clever arguments about God, His Son and His Spirit. The question of whether Jesus is the Son of God has been the topic of many debates all over the world and all through the ages. After all, it is a lot easier for our limited human minds to accept that He was just another prophet or an ordinary person.

Because the attacks on Christianity are becoming more and more fierce, we must pray every day that the Spirit will convince our hearts, that we will truly experience His presence and that we will believe in Him – the Savior – without a shadow of a doubt. We also have to pray, maybe even more so, that God's Kingdom will spread across the earth in an amazing way, that people will begin to repent and that His Majesty will prevail. Because we are sure of this one thing: there will come a day when every knee will bow before the risen Christ.

In the run-up to the commemoration of His coming to earth, let's take hands as believers and pray for the hearts of every single child of God.

Jesus, Son of God, I know that You are my Redeemer. I know that You are God! My God. Amen.

See Heaven

So we fix our eyes not on what is seen, but on what is unseen, since what is seen is temporary, but what is unseen is eternal.
(2 Corinthians 4:18)

When Jesus, the Son of God, was on this earth He often had reason to lose courage. After all, people did not believe Him, they doubted His message, there was an uprising against Him, they deceived and denied Him and ultimately they nailed Him to a wooden cross. And yet He remained absolutely faithful to His Father through it all, because He looked past the here and now and fixed His eyes on heaven.

When problems and setbacks seem to get the upper hand in your life, remind yourself of how Jesus stayed faithful to His Father and how He constantly focused His gaze on God. And then take these last words of His to heart: "And surely I am with you always, to the very end of the age" (Matt. 28:20).

May you get up off your knees with renewed courage today, knowing that God is constantly watching over you and that He is awaiting you in His new world.

Thank You for being there for me, Holy God. Amen.

Christmas Shopping

And so we know and rely on the love God has for us. God is love.
Whoever lives in love lives in God, and God in them. (1 John 4:16)

Christmas is creeping up on us – advertisements for Christmas shopping ideas are everywhere and shops especially play Christmas carols so as to make us sentimental and get us to buy even more. In the hurry-scurry of it all, you may not have time to keep to your spiritual schedule. And so your heart becomes emptier and emptier while the shopping carts only get fuller and fuller.

Maybe you should ask yourself how much of the worldly shopping you really need to do? Also think about what you can leave out so that you have more time and energy to spend on those things that will fill up your heart as well as other people's hearts.

This Christmas, try filling the Christmas stockings in the hearts of those around you with something different. How about a thank-you letter to show appreciation, a card with encouraging words or a God-loves-you-because … list? Or how about giving Bibles as gifts? In this way, you will be placing gifts with eternal value under other people's Christmas trees.

This year, decide to fill other people's as well as your own heart with gifts that have eternal value. Everyone is going to love it!

Lord, show me which gifts with eternal value I can give this year. Amen.

Go to Bethlehem

So they hurried off and found Mary and Joseph, and the baby, who was lying in the manger. (Luke 2:16)

You have probably heard the Christmas story of Jesus' birth a thousand times over. And you've sung along to the most beautiful Christmas songs from the top of your lungs. But have you ever been to Bethlehem yourself?

Have you ever really imagined walking through the dusty streets of old, coming up on the door of the stable and knocking before going in and sitting down on the hay with Joseph and Mary? Have you dared to go near the Baby in the manger, to reach out to Him and to let Him take hold of your little finger with His hand? Have you ever really felt His love for you?

Decide to go and meet Jesus in the manger this year. Allow Him – the great God – to take your hand. See His eyes filled with love as He looks at your face and hear the compassion in His voice as He tells you: "I came to earth for you, dearly beloved, so that you will never ever perish."

This year, kneel at the feet of the Baby in the manger.

Savior, I worship You, honor You and thank You for Your indescribable grace! Amen.

DECEMBER 13

Kneel before Him

On coming to the house, they [the Magi] saw the child with His mother Mary, and they bowed down and worshiped Him.
(Matthew 2:11)

This Christmas month, will you have the courage to kneel at the manger with the baby Jesus in it? Or are you scared? Scared of His judgment, punishment or retribution? Maybe you just don't have the boldness to do so, because you – typically female – feel so guilty about so many things.

At Christmas time, Jesus sends out a special invitation to all of us to come and kneel before the Son of God again, in spite of our brokenness, sin and debt. He wants to remind us that He came to earth, not for those people who always do the right thing, but for those who make mistakes and are sinful.

This is a time of celebration; a time to fall at the feet of our Messiah and to shout for joy because He is our Savior God!

Don't shy away from the welcoming arms of our Savior. He does not receive perfect people. No, He is waiting for imperfect ones like you and me.

Dear Savior, thank You for accepting me and loving me just as I am. Thank You for grace in the place of grace already given! Amen.

Start Celebrating So Long

Then Jesus declared, "I am the bread of life. Whoever comes to Me will never go hungry, and whoever believes in Me will never be thirsty."
(John 6:35)

Our Savior came to earth with one goal in mind. To make us – you and me – His children. That is why Christmas time also reminds us of another event: when a Man died on a cross so that we can live for all eternity.

The question remains: have you told this Man that He is your Lord and your God? Have you knelt at the foot of the cross to receive the salvation that He offers us unconditionally?

During this festive season, make the Christ, the Man on the cross, the One sitting on the throne next to His Father your own. Praise and thank Him for the fact that you can one day celebrate with Him forevermore.

Kneel at the cross and start your joyous
celebration now – the joy of being set free.

Thank You, Jesus, thank You that I can walk away from the Cross with joy in my heart. Amen.

Go and Look at His Grave

Suddenly Jesus met them. "Greetings," He said. They came to Him, clasped His feet and worshiped Him. (Matthew 28:9)

It was still dark when Mary and the other women walked to their Master's grave with sorrow-filled hearts. If only they could embalm His body that morning so as to touch Him one last time.

They were stunned when the heavenly beings told them that Jesus who had died on the cross, had risen from the grave and was alive! And then … He stands there in front of them Himself! And He says to them, "Do not be afraid" (Matt. 28:10).

Dear friend, the Lord is risen! He is alive! And that is what sets Him apart from others. He conquered both sin and death. And He did it all for you. What joy this brings us!

So, go and visit His grave this festive season. See the folded linen sheets and know that He was once there, but that He is now long gone; He has gone to prepare a place for you in heaven. May this also cause you to worship Him.

Thank You, Savior, that I can live forever through You. Thank You so much! Amen.

Receive His Great Power

But you will receive power when the Holy Spirit comes on you; and
you will be My witnesses in Jerusalem, and in all Judea and Samaria,
and to the ends of the earth (Acts 1:8)

God is just so amazing, isn't He? He answers without us even having to ask. He gives us breakthroughs in the most unexpected ways and even before we realize that we are in need of something, He has already provided it. Like giving us the Holy Spirit to equip us.

You can be assured of the fact that you will never find yourself ill-equipped when God prompts you in your heart to witness for Him.

If you are willing to obey Him and to do Kingdom work for Him, His great power will provide you with everything you need, from thoughts to words to actions. And so you will be capable of doing things far greater than your own abilities allow.

Never doubt yourself as you have the Holy Spirit in you.
He can do all things. And through Him – so can you!

Thank You for putting Your great power in me and that I can, therefore,
do what I need to do! Amen.

Look Past the Clouds

They were looking intently up into the sky as He was going, when suddenly two men dressed in white stood beside them. "Men of Galilee," they said, "why do you stand here looking into the sky? This same Jesus, who has been taken from you into heaven, will come back in the same way you have seen Him go into heaven."
(Acts 1:10-11)

Can you imagine how shocked and abandoned the disciples must have felt when they saw their Teacher disappear into the clouds? They were probably thinking: "What now?" And then the two angels stood there and put their doubts and fears into words: Do you think that you will never see Jesus again? Fortunately, the angels also have a reassuring answer: "This same Jesus, who has been taken from you into heaven, will come back in the same way you have seen Him go into heaven" (verse 11).

Dear friend in Christ, look up. See Jesus at the right hand of the Father, interceding on your behalf. Be assured of the fact that He will return to come and take you to Him. Until then … take courage.

Look up and praise your Father in heaven!

Dear Savior, thank You for preparing a place for me in Your eternal home. Amen.

Understand God's Calendar

*Be patient, then, brothers and sisters, until the Lord's coming.
(James 5:7)*

Have you also gone through times when you wished that Jesus would return earlier? After all, that would mean the end of all the pain and discomfort in this world. Just imagine how wonderful it would be to live in peace and love forevermore! Heaven means that we will be with our Father.

Through the ages, many people have made many predictions about when Jesus will return. But alas … we are still here! And that is because God's clock is different from ours!

In 2 Peter 3:8 Peter explains this to us when he writes, "But do not forget this one thing, dear friends: With the Lord a day is like a thousand years, and a thousand years are like a day."

One thing is certain: God will keep His Word. He will come back when the time is right. Until then, you and I are tasked with living out His Kingdom here on earth every day. Take heart, my friend!

Thank You, Lord of the universe, for the promise that You will indeed return. Help me to be ready for Your coming every day. Amen.

Wait for the Day of the Lord

The Lord is not slow in keeping His promise, as some understand slowness. Instead He is patient with you, not wanting anyone to perish, but everyone to come to repentance. (2 Peter 3:9)

I am often left speechless by God's boundless patience. How on earth can He remain patient with humanity while the greater majority is living like children of the devil? Just listen to and watch the news, we betray one another, we ruin each other's lives, we are destroying this beautiful world He created!

So, *why doesn't He just put a stop to it all?* we can't help but wonder. The answer lies in the Word where Peter writes: "Bear in mind that our Lord's patience means salvation" (2 Pet. 3:15). Our Father wants every single person on earth to accept Him as their personal Lord and Savior, because He doesn't want even one person to perish. And that is why He remains patient with this world.

> Let's pray and live our lives in such a way that the world
> can see God in us so that they can come to repentance
> and conversion ... and so that He can return sooner.

Our Father in heaven, let Your Kingdom come. Amen.

Speed Up His Coming

You ought to live holy and godly lives as you look forward to the day of God and speed its coming. (2 Peter 3:11-12)

God's timing is perfect – just like Him! So, we can be assured that He won't be late for His second coming. It will happen at the perfect time. In the meantime, there are some things that we can do:

- we can strive to do His will all the more every day and in doing so we will show the world that we belong to Him, and
- we can make use of every opportunity to spread the gospel.

When we live according to His will and work to expand His Kingdom, we are actually hastening the day of God. Because as soon as He is satisfied that every person on earth knows about Him, He will return. So, we must not waste any time to proclaim the good news to the world.

What can you do today to speed up the
coming of our Lord Jesus Christ?

Great Lord, I am so looking forward to Your return. Show me what I can do to bring others into Your Kingdom. And then help me to walk faithfully in my calling. Amen.

Live without Fear

For physical training is of some value, but godliness has value for all things, holding promise for both the present life and the life to come.
(1 Timothy 4:8)

Are you afraid of dying? Or are you actually looking forward to the day that you will find yourself in your Father's arms?

Napoleon Bonaparte said, "I die before my time, and my body will be given back to the earth to become food for worms." Job's words stand in stark contrast to this as he says, "I know that my Redeemer lives, and that in the end He will stand on the earth. And after my skin has been destroyed, yet in my flesh I will see God" (Job 19:25-27).

As children of the living God, we don't have any reason to fear death. And therefore, we can also live without fear!

Isn't it wonderful to know that we can look forward to heaven?

Thank You, great God, for leading me safely to You. Amen.

DECEMBER 22

Honor His Majesty

Give thanks to the God of gods. His love endures forever.
(Psalm 136:2)

The fact that our Lord is so close to us and that He lives in and with us every day, should never make us treat Him in an overfamiliar way. God is our Friend, but not our playmate; He is our Redeemer, but not a safety net for our sin; He is our Savior, and not just another person that needs our attention every now and then. God is holy and we must worship, honor and respect Him accordingly.

So, kneel down before His majesty every day and worship Him – for the wonderful way that He reveals Himself in your life. Praise Him for maintaining heaven and earth, while still meeting every seemingly insignificant need of yours.

See Him in the wonder of every sunrise and hear Him in the birds' singing. Feel His presence when you worship Him in His house and also when you commune with Him in the inner room of your soul.

God is too great for us to comprehend.
And yet He loves us with an everlasting love.
Let's honor Him for who and what He is.

Your majesty overwhelms me ... while Your Fatherly love gives me peace. Amen.

DECEMBER 23

Kneel at His Word

Your Word is a lamp for my feet, a light on my path. (Psalm 119:105)

It is wonderful that you are reading these devotionals, but remember: nothing can ever substitute the greatness of the Scriptures! Centuries after it was written, the Bible is still relevant, maybe even more so than ever before and we can apply its infinite wisdom to our everyday lives.

Read the Word when you feel discouraged and see how you are filled with hope. Search for answers in the Word when you don't know what to do and see how everything suddenly becomes clearer as you find answers and insight there. Cry your heart out as you seek comfort in the Word and see how He takes your pain away. Make the Word part of your life, let its wisdom guide you and let the truths of life contained in it become an integral part of who you are.

When you kneel before the Word of God on a regular basis, you will see how everything in your life will start falling into place. You will be surprised at the way it all comes together.

Make time to read the Scriptures and
you will be pleasantly surprised at
how God will guide your way day by day.

Make me willing to make Your Word an integral part of my life, please Father. Amen.

Accept His Gift

Thanks be to God for His indescribable gift! (2 Corinthians 9:15)

Tonight is Christmas Eve: an evening filled with festivities and everyone the world over is celebrating for various reasons. Many are just jolly because it's the festive season, others are looking forward to the party and for many of us it is a time of special family gatherings. The children are either expectantly awaiting Santa Clause who will bring gifts to fill their Christmas stockings or they can hardly contain their excitement at the prospect of opening the gifts under the Christmas tree.

The question is: how do you feel? Are you as excited as the children about the great Gift that your Father is giving you once again? Yes, dear friend, be filled with joy as you consider the wonder of His gracious Gift to all of humanity. Consider how very lucky we are that He sent His Son for our sakes – for your sake. Celebrate this truth in your heart and share the joy it brings with fellow believers.

May this year's Christmas Eve fill you with so much gratitude and joy that it causes you to spontaneously praise your Savior.

Thank You, great God, for sending Your Son to earth for my sake and that I can, therefore, come to You and stand before You having been cleansed of my sin. I praise You for this heavenly Gift that You have given me! Amen.

Really Celebrate Christmas!

But the angel said to them, "Do not be afraid. I bring you good news that will cause great joy for all the people. Today in the town of David a Savior has been born to you; He is the Messiah, the Lord. (Luke 2:10-11)

It is celebration time! The time to have peace in our hearts – in spite of all the unrest in the world. A day to have faith and hope for the future – despite all the unsolved problems in our lives. Today is a day to sing for joy. Because, child of God, your Savior came to earth more than 2000 years ago to redeem you … to save you!

This year, may Christmas Day be different for you because you have made the truth of the gospel your own; because you realize once again that you have so many reasons to celebrate and because you know that you will live in glory for all eternity – thanks to your Savior!

Sing with the angels in heaven today: "Glory
to God in the highest heaven, and on earth peace
to those on whom His favor rests" (Luke 2:14).

Hallelujah! I praise You! Amen.

Take Christmas Further

And I heard a loud voice from the throne saying, "Look! God's dwelling place is now among the people, and He will dwell with them. They will be His people, and God Himself will be with them and be their God." (Revelation 21:3)

Christ's coming to earth changed our lives forever. The day that He was born, God Himself came to live among us … His Spirit came to indwell us. We can follow His lead and live in His peace, because the Holy Spirit has such a very close relationship with us. We should listen to the Spirit's whisper guiding us every day – that is how we will know what His will is so that we can obediently do what He asks us to.

We can take the joy that the Baby Jesus in the manger brings us along on our journey of life and that means we can celebrate Christmas every day. And, therefore, we can – and must – strive to grow stronger in the faith day after day.

"How dangerous it is for our salvation, how unworthy of God and of ourselves, how pernicious even for the peace of our hearts, to want always to stay where we are!" writes François Fénelon. May you grow in the grace of your Savior every day.

Lord, help me to grow in and through You. Amen.

Remain Rooted in Him

So then, just as you received Christ Jesus as Lord, continue to live your lives in Him, rooted and built up in Him, strengthened in the faith as you were taught, and overflowing with thankfulness.
(Colossians 2:6-7)

"God loves you just the way you are, but He loves you too much to let you stay that way," said Fulton Sheen. There is only one way to live as a new person and to grow your faith every day and that is by having a personal, intimate relationship with Jesus Christ – being anchored in Him like the roots of a tree in the ground.

Now, we all know that there are some days when we succeed in living closely connected to God … just to have the winds of life blow that connection with Him away the very next day. The world just has a way of pulling us away from God.

That is why we need to possessively keep watch over our quiet times, when we get to read the Word and have intimate conversations with Him through prayer. We also need to cherish the times that we worship Him with other believers.

Pray every day that His living waters will fill you to the brim and that His love will strengthen your faith.

Keep me rooted in You, heavenly Father. Amen.

The Courage to Remember

"If you then, though you are evil, know how to give good gifts to your children, how much more will your Father in heaven give the Holy Spirit to those who ask Him!" (Luke 11:13)

It is time to reflect: it is that time of the year when we can't help but to recall all the highs and lows of the past year. Some of us had to go through times of great distress, sadness and pain. Others can savor memories filled with joy and heavenly glory, while most of us cast our minds back to a mixture of good and bad.

If you're honest with yourself, you'll admit that you survived this year because your ever-faithful Father was so very good to you. Think back on all the times when He gave answers even before you had asked; when He picked you up after you fell; when He comforted you in your sadness and the blessing of joy He let rain down on you time and again.

Yes, this year God was by your side the entire time, He is right next to you now and will still be there when tomorrow comes.

Thank You for always being with me, heavenly Father. Amen.

Be Happy and Grateful

... through psalms, hymns, and songs from the Spirit, singing to God with gratitude in your hearts. (Colossians 3:16)

The pressures of life, people and circumstances have a way of stealing our joy and gratitude from us. You can, however, refuse to give it up by – despite everything and everyone – living with a grateful heart that seeks to honor God at all times. Yes, when we are able to thank and praise our heavenly Father in all circumstances, a kind of divine peace, that nothing and no one can take away from us, settles in our hearts.

I hope that you will find time – or make time – to write a list of all the things that you are grateful for. A list of things for which you want to thank your Father. Set some quiet time aside and allow His Spirit to remind you once again of His amazing grace, His indescribable love as well as the many ways in which He has spoilt you with blessings over the last year. Then a deep-rooted feeling of everlasting joy will find its way into your heart.

A person's happiness depends on how
grateful she is. How happy are you?

Savior God, my heart bows down before You in grateful praise. Amen.

Feel His Faithful Love

Then come, let us go up to Bethel, where I will build an altar to God, who answered me in the day of my distress and who has been with me wherever I have gone. (Genesis 35:3)

The year has drawn to a close. You look back and realize that God never left your side, not even for one moment. Once again, He has proven to you just how much He loves you, that He wants to bless you and shower you with His goodness. How blessed are you to be His beloved child!

On this day may you quietly reflect on how great your God is, remember how He listened to you, how He made a way for you and how He was with you when you felt hopeless. Know that He is firmly holding your hand, ready to walk the rest of your life's journey alongside you.

Close your eyes and feel how His arms of
faithful love fold around you as He whispers:
I will be with you all the days of your life.

Great God, I worship You. And I love You … now and always. Amen.

Be His Bride

Then I saw "a new heaven and a new earth," for the first heaven and the first earth had passed away ... prepared as a bride beautifully dressed for her husband. (Revelation 21:1-2)

None of us have even the faintest idea of how wonderful and glorious heaven will be. Our wildest dreams don't even come close to visualizing God's greatness and beauty. All we know is that our life with Him will be breathtakingly wonderful.

Let us resolve to live the year ahead with joy in our hearts, to believe with an expectation and to tackle each day with renewed conviction and courage. Let us kneel before our Groom and ask Him to cherish us like a bride in the year to come. Let's pray that He will cleanse our hearts to look like a white wedding gown; that He will softly shower us with blessings and that He will give us all we need for the year ahead, tied up like a bride's bouquet.

May you end this year with peace in your heart because you know: Your Bridegroom watches over you 24/7 and awaits You in His brand-new heaven.

Here's my heart, Lord ... You may have it forever and ever. Amen.

A final thought
Take courage, dear heart!

… whatever you do, whether in word or deed, do it all in the name of the Lord Jesus, giving thanks to God the Father through Him. (Colossians 3:17)

My hope is that by reading through this devotional, you have been inspired to live with more courage. I pray that you were strengthened spiritually, that you discovered new horizons and that you have lived and will continue to live with greater expectation.

May you, strengthened by His power and filled with His peaceful love, start the new year with renewed hope, knowing that He will be by your side every step of the way. He will never leave you and one day … He will be waiting for you at the gates of heaven.

~ Milanie Vosloo

About the Author

Milanie Vosloo is a best-selling South African author who has positively impacted thousands of women's lives. Her complete honesty has touched the heart and soul of many readers, inspiring them to not lose hope.

By reading her books, you might just find that her sincerity, wisdom and life experience as a dynamic businesswoman, author, wife and mother, will positively impact your life, too.